Dedication

I dedicate this book to my beautiful daughter Jade. You inspire me as you "stir up the gifts" on the inside of you! May you continue to walk in the "Purpose" for which you were created before you were even conceived in my womb.
You are a world changer!

I0149100

STIR UP THE GIFT

The Journey to Fulfilling Your Purpose in Life

Deborah G. Hunter

HUNTER ENTERTAINMENT NETWORK

Colorado Springs, Colorado

Stir Up the Gift
The Journey to Fulfilling Your Purpose in Life
Copyright ©2017 by Deborah G. Hunter
First Edition: April 2017

Originally published under "Raising Your Prophet: The Journey to Fulfilling Your Purpose in Life" Copyright © 2006, Revised 2007.

To order products, or for any other correspondence:

Hunter Entertainment Network
4164 Austin Bluffs Parkway, Suite 214
Colorado Springs, Colorado 80918
Tel. (253) 906-2160 – Fax: (719) 358-9051
E-mail: contact@hunter-entertainment.com
Or reach us on the internet: www.hunter-entertainment.com
"Offering God's Heart to a Dying World"

This book and all other Hunter Heart Publishing™, Hunter Heart Kids™ and Eagle's Wings Press™ products are available at Christian bookstores and distributors worldwide.

Chief Editor: Gord Dormer
Book cover design: Phil Coles Independent Design
Layout & logos: Exousia Marketing Group www.exousiamg.com

ISBN: 978-1-937741-32-7
Printed in the United States of America.

STIR UP THE GIFT

The Journey to Fulfilling Your Purpose in Life

DEBORAH G. HUNTER

Acknowledgments

I want to truly thank all of those God has assigned and designed to encourage, equip, exhort, and empower me to walk in the fullness of God's calling upon my life. You all were a pertinent piece to the puzzle of my purpose. Thank you all for your obedience. May God bless you as only He is able!

Special thanks to a dear person that God has placed in my life during this season. An intercessor, a warrior in the Spirit, a woman that holds me in her arms in the Spirit, and covers me in warfare…

Lori Bleiweiss-Medina

… you inspire me with your love for humanity, your eyes and ears in the Spirit, and the *mothering anointing* that is upon your life. Although you have not birthed natural children, God is making you a "Mother to the Nations!" This is not the end, but just the beginning! Let Him *Stir Up the Gift* within you!

Table of Contents

Introduction

Growing up, I always wished I would have a little girl when I got married. I pictured in my mind how she would look; long, curly hair, big brown (or green) eyes, tall and thin like a model. I could see myself brushing her hair and putting bright, pretty bows everywhere. I could see myself dressing her in cute little dresses with pretty sandals to match. I thought of many names from Amber to Zoe. My heart filled with joy every time I thought of her.

My childhood was a good one. I was the fifth of six girls. We had good times and then some bad times, but overall, I enjoyed my days growing up. Having four older sisters made it easier for me and my younger sister to adapt to life through their experiences; some good and some, well… not so good.

My childhood came to a screeching halt at the age of fourteen. My father was diagnosed with lung cancer about two years earlier, which spread into his brain causing massive brain tumors. My world, as I saw it then, was crashing in all around me. I loved my father dearly. Every time he would get into his truck to go somewhere, I would jump right in beside him and fasten my seatbelt with a huge smile on my face.

There were not too many times that I was not right there beside him in that truck. I remember one night going to the drug store with my dad and one of my older sisters. I believe this was before we knew he had cancer? He complained a lot of his head hurting him, but just played it off with his sarcastic jokes, as usual. This particular night, my father pulled up to the drug store to get some medicine. When he got out, he went to the back of the truck and urinated on the ground completely out in the open. My sister became so angry with him saying, "Daddy, why did you do that? You are so embarrassing, I hate you!"

Well, being a teenager, this was normal behavior; nothing out of the ordinary. My father began to cry, which was something I do not ever remember seeing him do. He apologized and said that he did not know what he was doing, and all of sudden, he did not know where he was. This truly scared me, as well as hurt me, that he was going through this. I remember being so angry with my sister for the way she spoke to him. (Now I know that she did not mean him any harm; she was just being a "teenager".)

From that night on, I felt even closer to my father. Soon after, they admitted him into the hospital and they began treating the cancer with chemotherapy. He was in and out of the hospital for a while, becoming weaker every day. He lost his hair and lost a lot of weight. He still had his sense of humor, but you could see the light in his eyes growing dimmer with each passing day. It got to the point where he could not even talk or help himself any longer, so my mother admitted him into a Veteran's Hospice Center where he could be cared for intimately and where we, as his family, could spend quality time with him.

It was not too long before we celebrated his fifty-second birthday on June 12, 1988. We decorated his entire room with balloons and pictures of our family and sang *Happy Birthday* to him. He was in a lot of pain, but I knew God was with him. He died six days later on June 18, 1988. We were all there with him when he transitioned from this life. I remember clearly holding his hand tight and whispering in his ear that it was alright to let go. I was fourteen-years-old at this time, mind you. I did not know, at the time, where those words came from, but I do know now that his "Father" was awaiting him on the other side.

Several years earlier, he had given his life to Jesus, which led me and one of my other sisters to receive Jesus as our Savior, as well. Even though I did not really know the extent of what being *saved* meant, I felt God with me that very day in his hospice room. After everyone else had left the room, I went back in and removed our family picture off the wall and put it into his hand and proceeded to lie next to him for quite a while.

I felt closer to him at this point than I had ever before while he was alive. I am sure my family thought I was crazy for doing such a thing (nothing has changed), but as I look back, I saw God's hand over my father and I know that something was imparted into my life that very day. I was so peaceful. I was actually happy for him that he was no longer suffering and in pain. I knew deep inside that he was alright. I did not know this through intimate knowledge of God, but simply what I felt in that space of time.

The days following his passing were absolutely the worst of my life. The peace I felt that day in his room slowly turned to grief and mourning. I actually do not remember too much of the days leading to his funeral or the days after, but what I do remember was feeling like I could not breathe. I felt as if I, too, was dying. No one really talked much about him after his passing; everyone kind of went their own separate ways and fell silent. I was longing for something, some kind of reprieve, some sort of comfort… but I found none. There was no one to blame, as everyone was grieving in their own way.

I stayed in my room a lot thinking of him and how much life was on the inside of this man. I have to say that not once did I blame God for taking him, but I felt extremely alone. It became absolutely too much to bear; therefore, I tried to take my own life. Now some may ask, "How can you do such a thing if you knew God was with you?" I was only fourteen-years-old and after my father became ill, we had no one that took us to church, as he had done before. There was no comfort coming from my home, as it pertained to spiritual guidance. No one was telling me it was alright to grieve and that this was natural, because it felt anything but natural to me.

I hardly ever saw my mother cry at home after the passing of my father, but this is how she dealt with it. I do not fault her for this, because I was not the one who lost a lifetime partner; the father of her six children, but I needed someone to openly discuss how I was feeling. I was not receiving that, whether it was my fault for not asking or not anyone's, because we were all grieving, I cannot answer.

I came close to losing my life that day, but God had a different plan. I realize now that He had a purpose for me, as well as the lives of my future children. Jeremiah 1:5 states:

"Before I formed you in the womb I knew you; Before you were born I sanctified you; I ordained you a prophet to the nations."

About eight years passed after I had attempted to end my life when I returned to Christ. Eight is the number of "New Birth" or "New Beginnings". I did not know this at that time, but I realize now that God will take us through some things in our lives and allow us to look back on them, in order to see the significance of them. This same year, I delivered my first child; my little girl. She was exactly how I had envisioned her in my mind years before. She had long, curly beautiful hair, big brown eyes (she did not get my green eyes), and I could see from her arms, legs, and feet that she was going to be tall, just as I had seen her in my dreams.

We discussed many names, but the one that pierced my spirit was Aaliyah. My husband studied Hebrew culture for quite some time and decided that Aaliyah would be her middle name. This name means *going up* or *ascending*. While originally it referred to ascending to Jerusalem to celebrate the Jewish Feasts, today it has come to mean the return of the Jews to the Land of Israel. Aaliyah (Aliyah), simply stated, is the ingathering of the exiles from the four corners of the earth — it is the immigration of Jews back to their ancestral homeland. This name could not have become more prophetic in her life, as the enemy has tried many times to kill, steal, and destroy her, as well. God has proven faithful and revealed His mighty hand upon her life and I am seeing Him gathering many wayward children, prodigals, back into His bosom. We must trust His Word, His promises, and faithfulness to us, as we apply it to our lives.

> "Train up a child in the way he should go, And when he is old he will not depart from it." Proverbs 22:6

Her name meant even much more than this to me. A year earlier, I myself was diagnosed with cancer. I went through surgery to have the cancer removed, but they explained to me that I would never have an opportunity to have children. Oh the devil is a liar! I was devastated! I would never know the feeling of birthing a child. I would never know what it felt like to hold a child in my arms and to be called "Mommy". But the same way God had spared my life at the age of fourteen, He knew this was not His report for my life. He knew what would be birthed, not only through my natural womb, but what would come forth from the womb of my spirit! Needless to say, God has blessed my husband and me with three healthy, beautiful children.

> "That the word of Isaiah the prophet might be fulfilled, which he spoke: 'Lord, who has believed our report? And to whom has the arm of the Lord been revealed?'" John 12:38

I am here to testify that I am a living witness! I believe His report, as He has proven it time and time again throughout my entire life. And He has so graciously extended and revealed His arm, His Son Jesus Christ, in my life. From an encyclopedia of doctor's reports from hundreds of doctor's visits as a child, an attempted suicide, several bouts with cancer, rebellion as a teenager that led to me almost being murdered, to many other attempts of the enemy to kill, steal, and literally destroy my life, I am thoroughly CONVINCED that God's hand has been divinely resting upon my life. There is no doubt in my mind that He has a plan that far exceeds anything my natural mind can fathom, and every experience I have gone through in my life is simply a piece to that puzzle.

He has placed gifts within each of us and given us the grace to carry them out for His glory. Not one of us possesses the exact same qualities, characteristics, mannerisms, or attributes. And each of us has a life journey that not one other person has experienced. Though it may be similar to others; only you can share your story, your testimony. I want to encourage you today to embrace your experiences. Don't demonize them, or allow others to do so, because it is a part of your life experience, and God desires to use it all to bring many others into the Kingdom. Allow Holy Spirit to "stir up the gift" of God within you. Know that you are a vital key to the fulfillment of God's Will in the earth and the enemy knows this very well. He desires to hold us hostage to our pasts and to keep us in bondage to the things that have happened to us (to kill, steal, and destroy). God has come to heal us, deliver us, save us, set us free, and to give us *life* and *life more abundantly*! But He is not finished there. He doesn't merely bring us out; He has someone else on the other side of our freedom waiting to be freed from their prison, as well.

You are vital in God's plan of redemption for the earth. You are no longer a slave to sin, or even to your past; you are a *son*, redeemed by a loving and faithful Father. He has a plan already mapped out for your life and desires you to partner with Him to bring many others to His saving knowledge. *Stir Up the Gift* inside of you today!

1

The Preparation

Many times throughout our lives, we go through situations we feel are unfair and tend to ask, "Why is this happening to me?" or "Why do I have to go through this?" I have come to understand through my experiences thus far in my life, that they were all designed and absolutely necessary for me to be where I am at this very moment. Nothing that has ever happened to me was hidden from God. He has a master plan for my life and I have come to trust that even if I experience something *bad*, He will ultimately turn it around for my *good*. Jeremiah 29:11 is a favorite scripture of mine:

> "For I know the thoughts that I think toward you, saith the Lord, thoughts of peace, and not of evil, to give you an expected end."

Now the key word in this scripture is *expected*, which means to look forward to the probable occurrence or appearance of; to consider likely, or certain. The Hebrew word is *tiqvah*, which means *a cord (as an attachment); expectancy, expectation, hope, live, or thing that I long for.* God creates us with an expected end; already mapped out by Him. He longs for you to be what He created you to be and because of that, He has you on a "cord," if you will. Even though we may take a few wrong turns down the road, if you lean to Him,

He will get you back on the right path. You are attached to Him and the only way He will leave is if you cut the cord that leads to Him. This is such an awesome thought that we are created with a purpose that no one can take from us if we allow the Creator to lead us. And within us, there will always be this *expectancy*, or longing, for more, because it is embedded in our spiritual DNA.

I will use my life, because this is what I know best. God created me with a unique purpose in mind before I was even conceived in my mother's womb. Even though I tried to take my own life, He still saw my *expected end*. Glory to God! God is not moved by our circumstances, issues, or ignorance. He is the same yesterday, today, and forevermore. Just because we fall short in our lives does not mean His plan for us ends. Psalm 119:89 says:

"Forever, O Lord, Your Word is settled in heaven."

What God says will happen in your life, will take place if you allow Him to be in control of it. After my father died and my attempted suicide, I shut down on the inside. You would think God sparing my life would turn me around, but I still had no foundation of Christ in my life. Nothing was meeting that need deep down on the inside of me.

From the age of fourteen to twenty-two, I lived a life of rebellion. I chose to surround myself with people who were going nowhere and who had too much time on their hands. Not having that father-figure in my life anymore led me to seek out love from wherever I could find it. I led a life of promiscuity for a while, seeking to fill that void in my life. I know many choose not to expose their past sins, because they worry about what people will think of them, but I serve a God who has delivered me from such torment! This is my testimony of His goodness in my life; His grace and mercy that He extended to me, His daughter.

Even though life may deal you a *bad hand*, God can and will turn it around for your good! Now during these times in the "streets," I allowed myself to be placed in many dangerous situations. Not only was I rebellious, but I was outright stupid, as well. I exposed myself to the "realities" of the streets. I could have very well ended up with some kind of disease, pregnant with a child I could not take care of, or even worse, dead. But in my mind, I did not care, because I still wanted my life to end.

My chance came one dreadful night in those very same streets I was running around in. I was raped and my life was threatened. I had never been worried about this happening to me before, because again, I wanted to die, but this was different, it was, indeed, my *wake-up call*. I remember pleading with God to save me from this mess that *I* had placed myself in and that I would go home and change. He heard the cry of my heart and spared my life, once again. Did I deserve to be raped? Absolutely not! Did I deserve to be spared? No, but God, by His grace and mercy did, and I am eternally grateful for it.

After this ordeal, I went back home and began a new chapter in my life. It was still shaky, because I did not have someone to guide me spiritually, but I was renewed, somehow, in my spirit. God was showing me that He was with me the entire time, from my father's death, to my suicide attempt, the cancer, and the rape. He was there with me during those uncertain times of "What do I do now?" It is awesome to look back on my life and "see" God's hand upon me, even though I really did not know Him intimately. God did not place me in those situations to teach me anything, because He is not that kind of God. James 1:13-14 says:

> "Let no one say when he is tempted, 'I am tempted by God; for God cannot be tempted by evil, nor does He himself tempt anyone.'"

When it says that God cannot be tempted, it also means that He does not teach us lessons by causing evil or allowing bad things to happen to us. This is Satan's work, as well as our own foolishness, but again, God will use what the devil meant for harm and turn it around for our good. Genesis 50:20 says:

> "As far as I am concerned, God turned into good what you meant for evil. He brought me to the high position that I have today, so I could save the lives of many." (NLT)

Joseph's brothers, in this text, conspired to kill him because of their jealousy, but instead sold him to the Ishmaelites who took him to Egypt. Even though God does not cause evil things to happen to us, He will allow them, so that we will be placed on the right path He initially intended for us. God will create a need for us, or create a situation in our lives that will cause us to end up in the exact *position* He needs us in to receive His blessing. He also allows certain things in our lives to take place, as to reveal His glory in and through them.

Every step of Joseph's life was in God's hand. After he shared his dream with his brothers, his life seemed to get harder. His father sent him out to a place called *Shechem* to see if his brothers needed anything, as they fed their flocks. *Shechem* is a Hebrew word for "place of burdens". Many times in life, God will pull you away from your comfort zone and send you to a place of *lack* or *loneliness* to show you what it is that He desires for you. Verse 14 of chapter 3 in Genesis says that Israel sent Joseph "out" of the Valley of Hebron to go to Shechem. The Valley of Hebron in Hebrew means "seat of association," revealing to us that Joseph's family was only a means of birthing him into this world, not his appointed place of assignment.

I can look back upon my life now and clearly see that my family, namely my father, was my "seat of association". He led me to Christ at the age of twelve and when he died, God saw where I was heading, but did not stop me, because He already knew ahead of time where I would end up. There was a testimony attached to my wanderings. God knew where Joseph would end up, as well. Joseph's brothers were not willing to see what God was doing in his life, so instead of going to Shechem, they traveled to a place called *Dothan*, which means "a place of enchantment, or conspiring; conjuring." God knew Joseph's brothers' hearts and what they had conspired to do, but did not stop them. Why? God created an *expected end* for Joseph and this was part of his pathway to that place.

Please know that the enemy will place people in your life that will try and stop you from reaching that expected end, or that assigned place, which has already been mapped out for you. But even more importantly are those that God Himself "assigns" to propel you towards your destiny! They will conspire against you, as Joseph's brothers did, to stop God's plan from unfolding in your life, but they cannot stop you, unless you allow them. They will talk about you and stir up lies about you, but you have to know that the battle is not yours, but the Lord's. You also have to keep in mind that this is not *personal*; don't become distracted with things and/or people that are designed to catapult you into the place God has divinely assigned for you to be, in order to bless you and use you in the furtherance of His Kingdom. It is *all* a part of His ultimate plan.

God sees everything in your life before it happens and "prepares" you for it. You may ask, "Why would such a loving God allow these things to happen to me?" "Why can't He simply make it all better?" If this were the case, we would have no reason to need God; to seek our Creator. Where would our *transformation* come from? How would our *character* be formed? Even more importantly, how will *His glory* be revealed in and through our lives? He desires to fight your battles for you, so you are able to continue on in faith and perseverance to the very end. He will even send people into your life to stop any evil from happening to you, as you journey towards your expected end. Genesis 37:21 says:

"But Rueben heard it, and he delivered him out of their hands and said, 'Let us not kill him."

See, though God allows "not so easy" means to get us where He needs us, He will be sure to protect us along the way. There will always be a "ram in the bush," as our Lord walks us through the storms of life. *Rueben* in the Hebrew means "to see ye a son". Reuben saw and even "heard" something that his brothers did not. God spoke to Reuben to spare Joseph's life. God will choose someone to intervene on your behalf to guide you in the direction that He needs you to go. The one being used may not even know why they have intervened, but God strategically places people throughout your life, so that His perfect plan will be accomplished.

Reuben encouraged his brothers not to kill Joseph, but to throw him into a pit instead, which is significant of, or similar to, the wilderness. Genesis 37:22 says:

"And Reuben said to them, 'Shed no blood, but cast him into this pit which is in the wilderness, and do not lay a hand upon him_that he might deliver him out of their hands, and bring him back to his father."

This is how I saw God delivering me out of the devil's hand. I look back now and can clearly see how many times the enemy tried to kill me, but he could not, because God said, "No!" The things God does allow the enemy to test us with are only a means of developing our character as *sons* of God, as well as our trust in Him. Just as He said to Satan concerning Job, "Have you tested my servant Job?" is the same way He is saying this to him about you.

It says in verse 24 of chapter 37 in Genesis that the pit was *empty* and without *water*. Water represents Holy Spirit in this text, so we see that Joseph was without the guidance of the Comforter, which we have been given freely by God. We know God was with him, but he must have felt very alone. Scripture does not say whether Joseph was praying or not, but we must assume he was, indeed, pulling on the strength of his God during this very trying season of his life. Genesis 37:25 states:

"And they sat down to eat a meal. They lifted up their eyes and looked, and there was a company of Ishmaelites, coming from Gilead with their camels, bearing spices, balm and myrrh, on their way to carry them down to Egypt."

Ishmaelite in Hebrew means "God will hear". God heard Joseph's cries from the pit and "prepared" a way out, and eventually, out of the wilderness, as well. God answered Joseph's prayers in a way we might not fully understand, but He was in control and knew the outcome of his life. No matter what you are going through in life, know that God is with you. He created a purpose inside of you before you were conceived and He will get you to that purpose if you choose to trust and follow Him, no matter what it *looks* like in the natural.

Many times, we choose not to follow Him; therefore, we experience the consequences of that disobedience, but His plans for us have not changed. We serve a merciful God and even if you fall one hundred times, He can and will still work it out for your good if you humble yourself, repent, and turn back onto the pathway of purpose for your life. I understand that many of us, if given the choice, would choose not to go back through much of what we have experienced before in our lives. We must begin to see that every trial brings us closer to our Father and every test leads us closer to developing the mind of Christ. If Jesus would have chosen not to go to the Cross, we would all be on our way to hell. Instead, we have a way to the Father; the way of eternal life!

Also know that whatever you may be going through is ultimately not only about your transformation, but also someone else's deliverance. Your pressing and selflessness may very well lead someone else to Christ, who pressed His way to the Cross for the entire world to be saved! Your beginning, no matter how good or bad, is *preparation* for your future. God is looking for a people that can overcome their circumstances in this world, so they can reach something that is *out of this world*!

Do not allow hardships to decide who you are and what your "lot" is in this life. God is more than able to raise you out from underneath the ashes and make you look as if nothing ever happened. The key is never to forget what He has done for you and to give Him the glory for it all, so you can use it as a testimony for others. Joseph ultimately ended up in position where his brothers had to bow their knees to him for their own survival. Through it all, Joseph maintained his love and trust in God and gave Him the glory for each and every *roadblock* along the way to the palace; his purpose.

Seek Holy Spirit on what it is that God desires for your life. Remember, when things seem to look their worst, this is when God is about to bring an *Ishmaelite* your way to lead you out of the wilderness and into the Promised Land. Be careful not to move out of the wilderness prematurely, because this is where God is developing and preparing you for the next level in your walk with Him. This position is absolutely necessary in your life. There is a process that we all must go through, in order to receive the promises of God. God is not mocked. He will not release anything into your hands, until He has found you faithful and mature enough to receive. Even more than this, He desires to receive the glory in and through your life for every bridge you cross and every mountain you move. Allow Him the glory due His name!

"I am the LORD: that is my name: and my glory will I not give to another, neither my praise to graven images." Isaiah 42:8

Don't reject the process of preparation in your life. The outcome is of far greater importance than temporary satisfaction. Generations will see the glory of God displayed through your life and reap the rewards of your obedience to the Father. *Stir up the Gift*!

2

The Power of Persuasion

We saw from the last chapter that God can and will use our *mountains* to prepare us for what He has in store for us. Many times, we feel as if the load is too heavy and that we can no longer bear the weight of our problems, but with God, you are more than able! Matthew 11:30 states:

"For my yoke is easy, and my burden is light."

After many years of experiencing trials in my life, I began to see the light in the midst of the darkness. My sister, in whom I experienced salvation with as a teenager, began to encourage me in Christ. I finally had someone who was speaking the Word of God over me, which made a lasting impression upon my life. She gathered together some of her church leaders and they came to my home to pray for me and taught me the Word of God.

I rededicated my life back to the Lord after eight long and painful years (eight being significant of new beginnings). She *persuaded* me through her own experiences how faithful God was in her life. I saw the happiness on her face and I desired that kind of peace in my own life. I now knew this kind of peace could only come from God, and God alone.

The word *persuaded* is defined as to induce to undertake a course of action or embrace a point of view by means of argument, reasoning, or entreaty; to cause somebody to adopt a certain position, belief, or course of action. The Greek translation of this word is *peithos*, which means *to convince*. She not only *persuaded* me, but *convinced* me there was nothing that caused her joy, but God. My own sister was the one God used to bring me back to Him and ironically, she was the one sister that I always used to get into crazy arguments with… look at God! My life began to change dramatically over the next year. I began to feel as if I had a bigger purpose for my life than what I saw in front of me. I met my husband Chris and a year later, our daughter Jade was ushered into the world.

There she was, a precious gift from the Lord Himself; an after-thought of the doctors who told me that I would never have children. She was actually real. I could see her, touch her, and smell her. This was the most joyful day that I can ever recall in my life. God had saved me from myself, and from every trial I had ever experienced, the ones I caused and the ones I had no control over, and gave me a new life. He wiped away all of my past sins and forgave me, allowing me to forgive myself and become delivered in the process. On top of all of that, He blessed me and my husband with the little girl I had always desired.

I look back at how awesome God showed Himself over my life. My circumstances did not change who He was and what He had purposed to do in my life. I was sold! By this I mean I was *persuaded* of His goodness and His mercy that He so graciously offered to me. I was beginning to see how real God was and that He truly loved me.

Many people go through their entire lives not knowing how real God is in their own life. They are cured of diseases, rescued from death, saved from disasters, and delivered from their oppressors, but never see that it was God working on their behalf.

People go through life believing they have the best luck in the world and this is why they have been spared from tragedy. They refuse to believe the Creator of the Universe is the One who is orchestrating these very events in their lives from taking place. It is such a sad thought that many people never come to know the love of God in their lives, because they refuse to acknowledge Him. It is easier for them to believe in luck than to believe in a loving and gracious Creator who desires for them to live the abundant life He created in them before they were even formed in their mother's womb.

We have to begin to set aside our transplanted beliefs of why we are here and how we got here, and allow our spirit to bear witness to us. We are all created with a spirit, a body, and a soul. We all have the *inner witness* on the inside of us that speaks to us ever-so-quietly. Unbelievers call it their *conscious*; believers call Him *Holy Spirit*. No matter what we call it, we all have Him on the inside, because we were created in His image and in His likeness. Genesis 1:27 says:

> "So God created man in His own image, in the image of God He created him; male and female He created them."

So it does not matter whether you believe it or not, you were created by God and He did place purpose inside of you. Many of us are walking through this life completely out of our purpose, because we have failed to get to know the One who created us. We pursue many different avenues in life to become successful (as the world sees it) and end up with material prosperity, but living a life of defeat, because we are out of our designed purpose. It would behoove us to accept the Truth into our lives, because He will save us from going through this life *unconscious* to the magnitude of our existence. I can only imagine how many people have lived their lives outside of the purpose for which they were created?

Can you imagine an inventor creating something so wonderful that would impact the world in such a profound manner, but when he finished creating it, it did not serve the purpose for which it was created? Can you imagine how disappointed he would be? This is how God feels when we are not walking in the purpose that He created us to walk in. We have to become *persuaded* that we are more than what the world says we are, or even who we think we are. We are not evolved from mere animals as some believe or zapped into this world through some cosmic phenomenon. We were created by a Loving Creator and formed with purpose on the inside. Genesis 1:25-26 states:

> "And God made the beast of the earth according to its kind, cattle according to its kind, and everything that creeps on the earth according to its kind. And God saw that it was good. (v. 26) "Then God said, 'Let us make man in our likeness…'"

So the Bible distinguishes between man and beast. We have to stop listening to the world's perspective and get back to the living Word of God, which spoke us into existence. All throughout Genesis chapter 1, the Word says that "God said" and it was so. That very moment of Him saying "Let it be so," your purpose received life; it is real and living on the inside of you. Now, because of sin, we are born into a world that does not accept our purpose, but this does not change the fact that it still exists. If you are like me, I grew up in church, but never knew what it meant to have a personal, intimate relationship with Jesus Christ. We went through the motions of going to Sunday school, Vacation Bible School, and attended bake sales and dinners in the fellowship hall, but we were so detached from the Word of God that there was no life in our purpose for existing.

I do not remember once our pastor encouraging us that we had purpose in life or that God had even created one in us. We have to see that having a personal, intimate relationship with Jesus is having a personal relationship with the Word, who is Jesus. This was never a revelation we experienced in the church. We cannot expect to find our purpose outside of the Word of God. We have to open up the Bible and meditate upon it both day and night, in order to receive revelation into our own lives.

Another significant aspect that was missing from my experience in church, as a child, was the operation of Holy Spirit. I never heard mention of Holy Spirit. I never heard my pastor say that he received revelation from the Word of God. Not saying that he didn't, but it was not evident in the teachings. We were not a church that spoke in our heavenly language (tongues). This was a church that would probably think you had some kind of demon in you if you spoke in this manner.

We have to be *persuaded* that there is more that God wants us to learn from Him than just merely reading a book. The Word says "the letter killeth, but the Spirit giveth life." (2 Corinthians 3:6) We have to be hearing from the Spirit of God, in order to know the direction in which He desires to take us. We are His children and He desires to lead us. Romans 8:14 states:

"For as many as are led by the Spirit of God, these are the sons of God."

Many people choose not to accept the full Godhead: Father, Son, and Holy Spirit, because there is something they are not willing to *give up* to God. They want to be *associated* as being a Christian, yet have not chosen to walk in the fullness of God. I had a beautiful and precious woman of God walk into my office one day and she asked me if there were any nice churches in our area. I began to share with her the ones I knew of and she asked me which one I attended. I explained to her that my husband and I were members of a church about an hour away and she asked me why we traveled so far if there were nice churches here. I told her we had been led by the Spirit of God to join this particular ministry and she became absolutely excited, because she recognized the

Spirit inside of me. Her spirit bore witness with my spirit. She left my office so full of joy and expectation. I noticed that day how Holy Spirit will operate in our lives to *persuade* others of His fullness.

There will never be a day on this earth that we will reach such a level where we can no longer receive something new from God, because His Spirit dwells within us. He is still very real, and living vicariously through us. Many think because Jesus died, we will never experience His fullness in the earth realm, but this is not Biblical. We are left with the promise of Holy Spirit who leads, guides, directs, instructs, and reveals the heart of God to us every day. We must push forward in our daily walk with the Lord, in order to reach the divine plan, or purpose, for our existence. We have to be *persuaded* above all else that nothing or no one can keep us from our purpose, no matter what our situation in life may look like. God loves you and will bring that purpose to pass if you will simply trust Him. Romans 8:38-39 states:

> "For I am persuaded that neither death nor life; nor angels nor principalities nor powers, nor things present nor things to come," (Verse 39) "nor height nor depth, nor any other created thing, shall be able to separate us from the love of God which is in Christ Jesus our Lord."

We have to have this confidence that whatever "life" deals us, it is just a means of preparing us for something greater. In this preparation, we should become *persuaded* that what God created us to do will come to pass, because He is God. When we become bold like this, God has no choice but to give us what we need to fulfill that purpose, because we are walking in faith. We know from Hebrews 11:6 that faith is the only thing that pleases our Father:

> "But without faith it is impossible to please Him, for he who comes to God must believe that He is, and that He is a rewarder of those who diligently seek Him."

If you go after God with all of your heart, He will give you what you ask of Him, because your heart has now been aligned with His. It is no longer your desires being released, but His Will at work in your heart. It is not enough to simply believe that He will do it; we have to activate that faith by moving out in expectation of receiving, as if it has already been done. We have to release our faith, in order to obtain the promises of God and this is where many fall short. We want God to simply drop everything right into our laps, *free of charge*... no faith required. God does not operate in this fashion. When God releases something, it is because faith was released. We also have to be *persuaded* that everything God does is in His perfect timing. He wants us to live abundant and prosperous lives, but He also desires for us to be mature enough to maintain that which He releases into our hands. He does not want us to lose anything through foolishness, immaturity, or greed. He is wisdom! He knew you before you knew yourself, and He knows what needs to change on the inside of you before He can release you in His purpose for you. We seek the "gifts," yet have not been prepared through the process to sustain them.

Therefore, whatever you are going through in your life right now, see it as a necessary step, in order for you to reach the promise of God for your life. Many will call these trials in life *times of darkness*, but I will have to strongly disagree. I had an e-mail sent to me not long ago and it spoke of how a college professor was speaking to his physics class about God. He said, "If God created everything, then God created evil and since evil exists and according to the principle that our works define who we are, then we can assume that God is evil?" One of his students chose to interject and said to the professor, "According to the law of physics, what we consider to be cold is in reality, the absence of heat. We have created the word *cold* to describe how we feel if we have no heat." He continued on saying that darkness is, in reality, the absence of light. Light we can study, darkness we cannot. "How can you know how dark a space is? You measure it by the amount of light present. Darkness is a term man uses to describe what happens when there is no light present." He ended by saying this, "Evil does not exist unto itself. Evil is simply the absence of good, or God. Evil is the *result* of what happens when man does not have God's love present in his heart. The professor, standing in amazement, sat down. The young man's name who quoted this_Albert Einstein.

There is light in every situation that you will ever face or go through in this life. There may be instances where that light may seem very dim or even non-existent, but that does not mean it is not there. You have to be *persuaded* above all things that God is for you and that His plan for you will succeed, no matter what! 2 Timothy 1:12 (emphasis) says:

"For the which cause I also suffer these things:
nevertheless I am not ashamed: for I know whom I have
believed, and am *persuaded* that he is able to keep that which I
have committed unto him against that day."

In this scripture, Paul is in prison; one of those *dark times*, but he is still encouraged, because he understood why he was going through this trial. He was *persuaded* that God's plan for his life would succeed, no matter what it looked like to others. God desires for us to trust and believe in Him and what His Word says, so that we may live victorious and prosperous lives here in the earth. We need to become sold out to the thought that we are His children and that He will surely take care of what is His. We have to become so *persuaded* of this that others will see us and believe in Him simply by witnessing faith in our lives alone. This is how powerful one witness can be in the earth. Matthew 5:16 states:

"Let your light so shine before men, that they may see your
good works and glorify your Father in heaven."

So again, whatever God has allowed to happen in your life, it is for a greater purpose and prepares you for the process of entering into His perfect Will for your life. There will be many times that God will send something or someone into your life to *persuade* you to stay on the right path, so that you will not move out of position where He desires to *stir up the gifts* within you. These gifts are not for your benefit alone, but to benefit the Body of Christ, as a whole. And before He fully releases you into them, there must be a process of being fully *persuaded* that He is the One to be glorified through them, not us. There is great responsibility in being used as a vessel for God, and He does not desire for us to fall into the temptations of them. Allow God to mold you into that bright light, so He is able to release those spiritual gifts He created within you to reach this lost and dying world for Jesus Christ. *Stir up the Gift!*

3

Producing Your Fruit

When I delivered my daughter Jade, I was still in the state of unbelief. After all I had gone through in my young life; I never expected to be a mother. The devil had tried many times to wipe me out and keep me from this very moment, but God had a different plan, indeed!

From the last two chapters, we saw how there is a process that we need to go through in order to receive the promises that God has for us. The wilderness experience, or the "preparation" period in our lives reveals our weaknesses and allows us to become humbled before God, in order for us to see that we desperately need Him in our lives. These experiences provide us with a testimony, or witness, to be effective in the times ahead, because we will continue to go through trials in this life. As we look back, we see that if God delivered us from that, then He is more than able to do it again.

We saw that becoming "persuaded" about God's purpose for our lives gives us a boldness that is necessary to show the enemy that he can do whatever he chooses, but God has already received the victory and glory in our lives. This *persuasion* period ushers us into the "Producing" season in our walk with the Lord. Being persuaded means that you have faith that God is going to do what He said He would do in your life. No one can tell you any different, because you have testimony to back it up. Hallelujah! We understand that faith is what pleases God and without faith, it is impossible to please Him. (Hebrews 11:6)

Therefore, as we please Him, He begins to release those things He had to withhold from us during our *preparation* stage. We are now *producing* fruit in our lives for the glory of God. The Fruit of the Spirit is formed within our lives, as we submit and surrender to the Will of God in our lives. As we remain and abide in His presence, we begin to produce the life of Jesus Christ in and through our lives.

> "I am the vine, you are the branches. He who abides in Me, and I in him, bears much fruit; for without Me you can do nothing." John 15:5

It is always important to humble ourselves and to give God the glory for everything that is good in our lives, as well as the *not so good*, as it produces the greater character and transformation needed to carry out His perfect Will in and through our lives. In the beginning stages of a Believer bearing, or *producing*, fruit; we see an overflow of thanksgiving for His faithfulness in our lives. But many times, we get so caught up in the blessing that we lose sight of the One who blesses us. Remember, without Him, we can do nothing! This is very dangerous, because it can and will drive you right out of the Will of God for your life. Don't compromise the *preparation*, and subsequent *producing*, God has formed within you through pride or arrogance. Your fruit will begin to show signs of rottenness and this does not glorify the Father. Our goal in *producing* should always be to show, or reveal, the glory of God to others. John 5:8 says,

> "By this my Father is glorified, that you bear much fruit, so you will be My disciples."

This *producing* stage of our lives is not for us, but for others. It is pertinent to understand that much of what God releases into our lives is not for our personal benefit, but to bless and encourage others in the faithfulness and goodness of our Lord. Too many are teaching that "fruit" is the manifestation of physical things: money, cars, houses, businesses, or ministries, but the true fruit derives from the Spirit of God and its presence in our lives creates open doors that are far greater than anything physical we can possess in this life. Galatians 5:22-23 reveals the authentic fruit God desires to form in our lives:

"But the fruit of the Spirit is love, joy, peace, longsuffering, gentleness, goodness, faith, meekness, temperance: against such there is no law."

Many people go through their *preparation* process longer, because they fail to see the heart of God. Instead, they see what they want to see and follow the desires of their flesh and not the leading of the Spirit. God does not bless us, because we absolutely deserve it, because we absolutely do not! He blesses us to be a blessing to others and to do so, we must "house," or *possess*, the Fruit of the Spirit, which is ultimately the heart of our Lord and Savior Jesus Christ. He releases His divine plan for our lives when we obey His voice and endure the process of preparation with a willing heart and with knowledge that He has a plan and a purpose for our lives.

We also must understand that we do not get to choose our paths when we give our lives to Christ. In surrendering to His Will, we lay down claim to choose our own paths in life. Our lives are no longer our own, and therefore, we submit to His sovereign Will, because we understand that it is for His greater purpose. John 15:16 states:

"You did not choose Me, but I chose you and appointed you that you should go and bear fruit, and that your fruit should remain, that whatever you ask the Father in My name, He may give you."

Many take this scripture out of context by insisting that *whatever* we ask, God will give us. But this is truly heresy. This implies that we can live any kind of way we choose and expect a Holy God to "fulfill" our requests. This is NOT prayer, and this is NOT His Will! This, in reality, is witchcraft! It is trying to manipulate God to give you what you want, without submitting to His perfect Will for your life. The goal is to be transformed from our *old man*, into a *new man*, or new creature. So we are being formed day by day into His image and His likeness. In this, He places His Will within us through the power of Holy Spirit. Now, as we ask of Him, it is no longer selfish or self-centered prayers, but our will being lined up with His Will for the ultimate glory of God.

The time of bearing, or *producing*, fruit is appointed by God Himself, not our timetable. *Appointed* is defined as fixed or established, especially by order or command. God commands for our fruit to come forth when it is ready to come forth, and not until. We see in the world things obtained faster than we see in the Kingdom, because in the Kingdom, God is purging us of "self". He is removing those things that will hinder us from walking in His Spirit; those things that will cause us to compromise our faith for the *promises of this world*. The world is used to getting what they want at any cost. They will walk over people and use others to get the things they desire. They will lie, steal, cheat, and yes, sometimes even kill to obtain the *riches of this world*, but this is not *producing* the fruit that God has commanded, and willed over your life. Ezekiel 17:9 states:

"Say, 'Thus says the Lord God: "Will it thrive? Will He not pull up its roots, Cut off its fruit and leave it to wither? All of its spring leaves will wither and no great power or many people, will be needed to pluck it up by its roots."

So we have to be *persuaded* that seeking the "fruit of the world" only leads to destruction. We should desire the fruit that is eternal. Many believers begin their Christian walk with the teachings of this eternal fruit, yet end up being carried away by the lusts of the flesh. So many fall into the temptation of fast money and quick fame and end up forfeiting the true, authentic blessing of God for the Spirit of Mammon, a celebrity-like spirit that breeds pride, arrogance, notoriety, and greed. They have fallen into this glamorous lifestyle and are lured into believing they are being a light to "Hollywood," but are in reality, falling away from the Living God. They have failed to guard themselves and failed to separate from the stain of corruption and deceit. They have forsaken the humble and contrite spirit, the narrow path, and chosen the "high places," instead.

However, there are others that have held fast to the teachings of the Word of God and have trusted wholeheartedly in the process of preparation that God has seen them through, and understand that He will exalt them in due season and for His purposes, not their own. They have remained obedient to the leading of Holy Spirit and glorified the Father throughout their journey. In their times of not being "recognized," they fully relied upon God, knowing they had a greater purpose in life than the applause of man. They have remained faithful and steadfast in their *wilderness* seasons, therefore giving them a testimony of His goodness, *persuading* them that He is the only way! Now, they are *producing* great fruit in their lives for the Kingdom of God.

The birthing process is a very exciting time in the natural, as well as the spiritual. *Birthing* is defined as the emergence and separation of offspring from the body of the mother. The Greek word for this is *omos*, which means to *experience the pains of parturition*. Before a child is birthed, a seed has to be planted. This seed begins to grow and mature during a nine month period before it can be released from its mother's womb. For it to be fully matured; brain, lungs, heart, and all other organs, it has to reach this nine month period of maturation, or at least very close to it. If it does not, the organs cannot function properly on their own, so the child has to be nurtured and cared for by alternative means, until the organs have become large enough for the child to be released to their parents.

It is very much the same in the spiritual. The seed is planted in us before we are even born. That seed, or plan for our lives, is watered throughout our lives in many different ways, through trials, experience, correction, and eventually, the Word of God. This is the incubation period, if you will, where our purpose is nourished, as a child is in his mother's womb. Just as a child can be born prematurely, our purpose can be hindered if we try to release it before its *appointed time*. Many of us, once we come to Christ, automatically assume we will be thrust into our purpose, but fail to realize the much needed process of transformation designed to free us from our worldly and carnal ways. We need to have our old ways of thinking erased and our minds renewed through Christ Jesus. Romans 12:2 states:

"And do not be conformed to this world, but be trans-formed by the renewing of your mind, that you may prove what is that good and acceptable and perfect will of God."

So, if we desire the fruit that will not fade away, we should be prepared to go through a process of transformation in our lives. Anytime that God releases the blessing in our lives, the enemy will come to frustrate and confuse. He will try every trick in his book to tempt you into becoming more interested in the blessing, than in covenanted relationship with God in Heaven; our Abba Father. We have to remain mindful of Satan's schemes and how he operates, so that we will not be pulled into his trap of temptation.

Please know that Satan hates when we bear the authentic Fruit of the Spirit. He will do everything in his power to kill, steal, and destroy the very work of Christ in our lives. He desires to corrupt it and deceive us into believing it's "not enough". Please understand that even though you may be seeing the fruit of your obedience, it does not mean the trials are over. More often than not, we see more trials come when we begin to receive the promises of God. For whatever reason, we find ourselves having to go back and go through something over again, but remain encouraged; God is simply taking us to new levels in our faith and *producing* even greater fruit in our lives. There is a test for every level God takes us to, and we must remain humble as we are promoted to higher levels of accountability and responsibility in Christ. We must go down before we go up. I believe this is another reason why Christians struggle in the church, because we fail to see the process, or seasons, God takes us through to release more into our lives.

We have a very real enemy and he is a twister of the Truth. He is a liar and the father of all lies! He tries to persuade us as well, and his goal is to get us as far away from intimacy with the Father as possible. He manipulates our thoughts and tries to make us believe God is some sort of tyrant for making us go through these "seasons". Why can't He simply release the blessing if He loves you? Why would a loving God allow you to go through hurt, pain, and disappointment before you can receive His promises? He wants to deceive us into believing we don't have to go through these things; therefore, offering us alternative ways to obtain the "promises". If you are *producing* fruit and have not had to go through any trials along the way, you need to ask yourself, "Am I in the Will of God?" He is not after our happiness; His goal is the Fruit of the Spirit produced in and through our lives for His glory! Again, the process of birthing is compared to this, because natural birth is very painful. The Word of God in Genesis 3:16 says:

"To the woman He said: 'I will greatly multiply your sorrow and your conception; In pain you shall bring forth children; Your desire will be for your husband, And he shall have rule over you."

At the moment your child is about to enter this world, it is probably the most painful experience one could ever go through. This is how your purpose should come to pass. To birth a promise, especially from the Lord, there is going to be some pain and struggle involved. If you do not travail in some manner before your purpose is established in the earth realm, then again, you need to ask yourself, "Am I in the Will of God?" We saw how even our Lord Jesus Christ had to endure excruciating pain during His process of getting to His promise. It hurt, but He knew the pain would be nothing compared to the lives He would ultimately bring alongside of Him, as well as the glory of the Father. The eternal reward was more important to Him, than the temporary afflictions He had to endure to get to the Promise.

This is how we should expect, as believers, to get to our purposes in this life. We have to be willing to go through some pain, affliction, and yes, even persecution to receive the *fruit* that God desires for us. The more we go through, the more He can get to us, because He knows that through our wilderness experiences, we will gain knowledge of what it means to possess *His fruit* and remain humble. As we press our way through these experiences, God will honor our obedience.

"And He will love you and bless you and multiply you; He will also bless the fruit of your womb and the fruit of your land, your grain, and your new wine and your oil, the increase of your cattle and the offspring of your flock, in the land of which He swore to your fathers to give you." Deuteronomy 7:13

Look at this! God tells us that He will bless the fruit of our womb. He does not say *possibly* or *maybe*; He says He will. What are you holding on the inside of you that God wants to bless? What do you possess on the inside that is ready to be birthed into the earth realm? Remember, God created each one of us with a unique purpose, gift, and we know He does not create out of mere existing; He creates out of purpose to impact the world!

I have had to go through this process several times in my saved life. It is surely not easy and, at times, very painful. God had to pull some things *out* of me, so He could put some things *in* me. I actually felt as if I was dying on the inside. This is the process of crucifying our flesh and this is not an easy thing to do, but if we are willing and obedient, God will honor it and walk with us through these painful, but necessary seasons.

> "If you are willing and obedient, You shall eat the good of the land." Isaiah 1:9

I was led directly into my purpose through this process and I do not regret going *through* to get *to* what God had for me. It was truly the best thing I could have ever experienced, as it built great character within me, formed me into His image and likeness, and established His perfect Will for my life. I am a changed woman due to the process of preparation in the wilderness seasons of my life. I do understand that I will continue to face adversity in this life. I am cognizant that God will move me into different seasons that require greater levels of brokenness and humility, and I am submitted and surrendered to that process. We have to be prepared for what God has ordained for our lives. Luke 12:48 states:

> "But he who did not know, yet committed things deserving of stripes, shall be beaten with few. For everyone to whom much is given, from him much is required; and to whom much has been committed, of him they will ask the more."

So, if you are in the race to finish, you'd better be prepared to go through some battles before you cross the finish line. We all know the finish line is eternity with our Father God, so expect to cross mountains, or *go through them*, as you begin to *produce* the fruit God desires for your life.

Many of us get past the *preparation* and *persuading* stages and begin to rejoice prematurely. Now rejoicing in each stage is a good thing, because it is a proclamation of God's goodness and faithfulness in your life, but make sure you understand that even after you begin to *produce* fruit, you will continue conquering the mountains of this life on your way to your Promise. There is never an *arrival* in this life. Far too many spiritual leaders are erroneously teaching people that there is this "bliss" here on earth. They teach more on what God will give us, instead of preparing believers for the wilderness seasons they will undoubtedly face in this life. This is devastating, because it is setting people up for failure and disappointment. God will bless us and wants us to prosper, but more importantly, He desires growth and stability in our lives. As we begin to *stir up the gifts* of God within us, we must look toward the purpose and not the temporary fulfillment of earthly blessing. Is He able to bless us abundantly, yes!

> "Now unto Him who is able to do exceedingly, abundantly above all that we ask or think, according to the power that works in us." Ephesians 3:20

This is probably one of the most exciting scriptures in the Bible! God is a good God. He is not a tyrant. He wants good things for His children. Exceedingly means *abundantly*, which means abounding with or rich; *above*, which means being or representing the entire or total number, amount, or quantity, wholly and completely; that we can ask or even think to ask of Him. This is so powerful! This shows us that God's thoughts of blessing us exceed our capacity to even think of how we desire to be blessed. We do not know how God desires to bless us. We limit the Father by settling for what the world views as "blessed". Again, this is only a temporary solution that does not bring joy into our lives. It merely medicates us and keeps us from the true joy of our purpose and assignment in the earth. *Stirring up the gifts* of God within us stirs up eternity in our hearts! It causes something amazing inside of us to rise up, and nothing in the world can satisfy it, except God.

The *birthing process* in our lives, spiritually, is connected to Kingdom purposes, not individual promotion. The fruit God produces in our lives continues to grow at each level and in each assignment He allows us to participate in. We grow exponentially, not merely for our benefit, but to be a blessing in the lives of those assigned to our lives and our assignments. He has great plans that we play a role in, and it is to advance His Kingdom in the earth. We hear so often the term *favor* in Christian circles, and let me tell you, it is a word that has been so misconstrued and abused for far too long. Often when I hear it, I cringe, because I understand it is manipulated greatly. God gives us HIS favor only in an effort for His plans to come to pass in our lives, as well as in the lives of others. It is not because we have been so faithful, or that His hand and anointing is so great upon our lives that favor *follows us*. This kind of thinking produces pride, arrogance, and yes, a spirit of entitlement that brings no glory to the Father. It is a selfish motive that seeks *tangible* things, instead of His Will coming to pass through us. When God releases His favor, you best believe it is because He has a plan that needs to be implemented, and the only way it will be able to, is because He has done it! God's *favor* is not for us to look good; it is to bring *Him* glory!

The *fruit* produced through this *birthing* season is extremely valuable. It is fruit that will last. It is fruit that no man can take from you. It is fruit that is eternal. It produces a trust in God that is immovable! Many years ago, I heard Holy Spirit reveal something concerning my financial situation that truly opened my eyes and tested my faith, at the same time. Holy Spirit said that my job was merely a place for me to be the *light* He desired in the midst of darkness. He explained to me that the income I was receiving was not intended for my leisure or pleasure, but to sow into the Kingdom of God to bless and help others in need. Okay, you know I had some questions, right? First of all, I knew this wasn't the enemy, because he would never tell me to sacrifice finances to further the Kingdom of God or to bless someone else for that matter. The question I did ask was, "God, how then are we going to pay these bills?" I thought I was working to help pay off our debt. Holy Spirit led me to several scriptures, the first being Deuteronomy 24:19, 22:

"When you reap your harvest in your field, and forget a sheaf in the field, you shall not go back and get it; it shall be for the stranger, the fatherless, the widow, that the Lord your God may bless you in all the work of your hands." Verse 22: "And you shall remember that you were a slave in the land of Egypt, therefore I command you to do this thing."

Many times, we hoard our finances and they become an idol in our lives; therefore, causing God's hands to be tied over us, preventing us from receiving the release of more fruit. The definition of *hoard* is a hidden fund or supply stored for future usage. We are trapped in bondage by the enemy that tries to make us believe our jobs are all we have, and that we must hold on tight to these "things". We do not know what our future holds; neither do we live according to the precepts of this world. The world operates in the business of buying and selling; the Kingdom operates according to the law of sowing and reaping. If we, as Believers, want to produce greater fruit, then we must flow in the principles of Heaven and of the Spirit, so God can begin to *stir up the gifts* within us to advance the Kingdom in the earth.

The next scripture Holy Spirit led me to is Deuteronomy 26:12-13, which states:

"When you have finished laying aside all the tithe of your increase in the third year_the year of tithing_and have given it to the Levite, the stranger, the fatherless, the widow, so that they may eat within your gates and be filled," Verse 13: "then you say before the Lord your God: 'I have removed the holy tithe from my house and also have given them to the Levite, the stranger, the fatherless, and the widow, according to all Your commandments which you have commanded me; I have not transgressed Your commandments, nor have I forgotten them."

Holy Spirit revealed greatly to me the power of a giving heart and I realized God has an endless resource of blessing that He desires to get through the hands of the willing and obedient. When we hoard and when we worry about how we are going to take care of ourselves, our faith is stifled and we live in fear and bondage to money. When we trust God to take care of us, we understand that money is not our source and in grasping this revelation, we can begin to allow Him to *stir up the gifts* inside of us that will eventually produce more and more in our lives, for the blessing of others. We should desire a heart to give and to release out of us the beauty of the fruit the Lord has put inside of us. The least of this fruit is financial. It is encouraging others to walk in the full purpose of God for their lives. It is empowering others to live in the fullness of God. It is equipping others to walk out their God-ordained destiny and to *Stir Up the Gift* within them, as well, so they can go out and do the same for someone else! This is a direct result of the principle of Genesis 3, *to be fruitful, to multiply, to replenish, to subdue, and to have dominion in the earth.* God's desire is to produce *LIFE*! Life in every area, and in every form.

We must begin to understand that our gifts are for the encouraging, empowering, and equipping of others to live their best life possible in Christ Jesus. We must take the focus off of what God can do *for me*, and turn it around. What can God do *through me*? Remember, "... to whom much is given, from him much will be required." The last verse Holy Spirit led me to as He began revealing the *greater things* was Philippians 4:18-19, which states:

"Indeed I have all and abound. I am full, having received from Epaphroditus the things sent from you, a sweet-smelling aroma, an acceptable sacrifice, well pleasing to God. And my God shall supply all your need according to His riches in glory in Christ Jesus."

I began to see, as I surrendered and submitted to His leading, that He was taking care of every one of my needs. Something supernatural was happening in my life, and it was greater than me and my immediate circumstances. As I began to seek God for the needs of others before my own, He began to open doors of opportunity for His love to be revealed through me. It was no longer about my needs. As I began to seek the needs of others, God was behind the scenes working it out on my behalf. What a loving and faithful God we serve!

In the previous scripture, the word *need* is the Greek word *chreia*, which means *employment, affairs, demand, requirement, destitution, business, lack, necessity, use, or want.* As I obeyed the Lord when He was telling me that my job was not my source, and that it was a doorway not only for me to bless others financially, but to minister spiritually, He opened up a door that literally blew my mind! Immediately after this, Holy Spirit spoke to me to begin my publishing company. I was at a loss for words, because this was never my desire. I loved to write and by this time, I had self-published three books. But being a publisher was not on my radar. Not understanding then that this was simply a "piece" to the puzzle of how He would use me to help others to *Stir the Gifts* within them. When our sacrifices are pleasing to Him, and when our obedience is fulfilled, He will allow things to happen in our lives. He will allow you to continue to remain on that job that is speaking of lay-offs *and* promote you. He will open the door for businesses to be established. And He will supply all your need according to His riches in glory in Christ Jesus! His promises are true!

Our faith will grow day by day, as we walk with the Lord in obedience. He desires us to grow from faith to faith, and glory to glory. Meaning, we are not to remain stagnant and complacent in our spiritual journey. He has much more to share and reveal to us, and He also has much more for us to do for His Kingdom. The places He is taking you to will require *greater* faith and trust in Him. The enemy is unleashing havoc upon the world, and trying to hinder the cause of Christ in the earth, and that includes the attack on your faith. Remain and abide in the presence of God and continue *producing* fruit for His glory. Allow Him to birth within you His purpose and His promise. Make Him your priority and He will make all things work together for your good. Matthew 6:33 states:

"But seek first the Kingdom of God and His righteousness, and all these things shall be added to you."

I truly believe the reason many believers fail in the area of faith is because we have yet to renew our mindsets. Once we settle in our minds that God is our only source and that He will truly supply all of our needs and all we will ever need, then we will begin to see the release of His blessing into our lives. As we submit to His Will and partner with Him in His purposes, He will make sure to take care of what is His. He will never leave us or forsake us. He is our Daddy, our Abba Father, and He is Jehovah-Jireh, the Lord our Provider.

Allow God to *Stir the Gift* up on the inside of you. Let Him birth within you great and mighty things, so His glory can be revealed through you. Many of us have inspired gifts lying dormant inside of us, waiting to be released by God for the furtherance of the Kingdom. No matter what your gifts are, know there is a process of preparation you must go through, in order to walk in the fullness of God's purposes for your life. You will not begin to *produce* the fruit of your spiritual womb, until it is totally submitted to the Will of the Father. Do not despise the process and do not despise small beginnings. Understand that He is trying to prune you, so your fruit will remain, and that it will continue *producing* and that He can use you effectively in the furthering of His Kingdom.

"Every branch in Me that does not bear fruit He takes away; and every branch that bears fruit He prunes, that it may bear more fruit." John 15:2

Do not allow your gifts to be taken away. Do not leave this earth without realizing the gifts God has placed within your life. Do not go to your grave not fulfilling His purpose in you. You are a gift to the world and the gifts within you, many are awaiting their manifestation, so they, too, can recognize their own. *Stir up the Gift!*

4

Protecting the Gift

Once a person becomes a parent, natural instincts begin to kick in and we now have a desire to *protect* that newborn child from all harm. We sleep with "one eye open," if you will, to make sure they do not fall or to make sure they are still breathing (I know I am not the only one.) We have such a drive deep within us to *protect* them at all costs. And God forbid anything happens to them; you will see us turn into someone you never thought we'd become.

This is how we should be with the gifts God has given to us. We should set out to protect and shield our gifts from any outside dangers. Our enemy, Satan, does not want to see us fulfill God's purposes for our lives. His desire is to steal, kill, and destroy everything in our lives and leave us empty. He is out to destroy God's seed in the earth, both natural and spiritual, and it really begins with the family unit.

"The thief does not come except to steal, kill, and to destroy. I have come that they may have life, and that they may have it more abundantly." John 10:10

Satan knows that God places purpose inside of us before we are even formed in our mother's womb. His desire is to stop that purpose from manifesting in our minds and in our hearts. This is why we see so many abortions taking place in our world today. This is the work of the devil. He does not even want us to enter into the world, because he knows the impact we will have in the earth realm once we discover our God-given purpose.

In the United States alone, over 58,586,256 babies have been aborted since the formation of Roe vs. Wade in 1973[1]. In an April 2013 report, the worldwide total of abortions was estimated at 1.72 billion since 1973[2]. Now this is merely forty years of calculating worldwide stats. How many more children have been aborted or murdered throughout history? We know of the decree of Herod that was sent forth to kill all boys throughout Bethlehem and surrounding areas that were under the age of two-years-old in hopes of preventing the Messiah from being revealed. Abortion is a spin-off spirit of this very decree that was sent to destroy the seed of God in the earth realm. Just as we should pray earnestly that this spirit is eradicated in the earth, so, too, should we pray fervently for the spiritual gifts being birthed in and through us in this life. Our enemy not only hates it when we come forth through the womb, but he also despises the gifts within us that are designed to bring God glory and to bring others into the saving knowledge of Jesus Christ. He wants to destroy it all!

This is why it is pertinent to know how to protect the promises of God within us. Holy Spirit will lead us and guide us if we will simply allow Him to do so. We must seek to hear His voice, so He can instruct us in the way we should go. He provides strategies for us to guard ourselves against the attacks and temptations of the

[1] *58,586,256 Abortions in America Since Roe v. Wade in 1973.* Life Site News.com. http://www.lifenews.com/2016/01/14/58586256-abortions-in-america-since-roe-v-wade-in-1973/.
[2] *1.72 billion Abortions Worldwide in the last 40 years.* Life Site News.com. https://www.lifesitenews.com/opinion/1.72-billion-abortions-worldwide-in-the-last-40-years.

enemy. As we hide ourselves in His presence, He will protect us and keep us.

As I stated previously, the enemy's number one attack is on the family unit. He desires to destroy families, so that children will not realize their purpose in life. When families are destroyed, children suffer more than anyone else. Most feel like it is their fault why their parents get divorced. This eventually leads to self-inflicted torment for the child/children. Satan knows that if he can get to a child's mind early enough, he has a chance to crush the purpose on the inside of them. Strong family units are absolutely imperative to a child's emotional, spiritual, and mental development and well-being. I know many people today have adopted the world's views on how to raise a well-rounded child, but there was a master plan created by Father God and it included a father, a mother, and the fruit of their covenant, children. Some believe a single-mother, or single-parent, can raise a child just as good as a two-parent family. Now, many single-parents are doing this and many of the children do fine, but this was not God's plan for the family.

Fathers and mothers both have something uniquely created within them to be sown into their children's lives, in order for them to be all that God desired and created them to be. Some mothers were thrust into single parenthood for whatever reason and have had no choice but to raise their child/children on their own. But many women today choose not to have the father of their child/children in their lives for nothing more than selfishness, and this is detrimental to the success of their lives. We must understand that the moment we chose to bring a child into this world, it ceased to be about us and our wants and desires. We have to stop thinking about ourselves and begin to realize that God placed a purpose on the inside of that child and both father and mother play a role in the nurturing of the gifts within them. The absence of the father in a child's life is the single-most reason why children veer off from their life's purpose. The identity of a child rests within the DNA of their father. He possesses something within him that only he is able to impart into that child's life. Withholding that gift from a child's life is absolutely selfish and destructive. I have witnessed far too many women do this, thinking they have all they need to impart into their child/children's lives, but find out too late that it was, indeed, not enough.

Some mothers have no choice, as the father has passed away or a father that has abandoned his children. In this case, the best route to take is to allow that child to know as much "good" about their father as you can give to them. For some, that may simply mean knowing the name of their father, and that's it. In the most extenuating circumstances, this may not even be available. Only God will be able to impart into the life of a child, in this case. But it should be the utmost priority of a mother to cover the view their child has of their biological father, no matter what it takes. Because this doesn't happen in many cases, children are left to the vices of their minds to figure out their identity on their own. This is truly the enemy's playground. He loves to come in and twist a child's mind and to deceive them into believing they are something or someone they are not. We have seen the rise in homosexual, lesbian, transgender, and other alternative lifestyles in our world today. A child not knowing a crucial part of them causes them to seek their identity in other people and other things. A father's presence in their child/children's lives provides stability, discipline, and self-worth. This holds true for both boys and girls. It is by far the most important relationship in a child's life! I know I may get blasted for this statement, but even as a mother of three and a step-mother to three, I have realized this truth personally in my own life.

God's Word even speaks to the times we are living in today in Malachi 4:6, which states:

> "And He will turn the hearts of the fathers to their children, and the hearts of the children to their fathers, Lest I come and strike the earth with a curse."

God is pronouncing judgment here if we do not turn our society around. He did not say He would turn the hearts of the children to their mothers; He said He will turn them to their fathers. We cannot deny this truth. We must embrace the wisdom of God and trust that He knows exactly what we need, and apply it to our lives and the lives of our children. We have to *protect* the gifts and purpose on the inside of our children or Satan will surely lure them into his trap. We must become vigilant in the Spirit when it comes to our children's destiny. This is not a physical fight, but a spiritual one. We must go into warfare for the lives of our children to loose them from the grip of our enemy. This takes a lot of sacrifice on the part of parents, but God has entrusted us with them, so we must partner with Him to birth their gifts and purpose in them.

We, as parents, must first know Jesus Christ for ourselves. We must enter into a personal relationship with Him and find our purpose in life before we bring children into the world. It is never His desire to work backwards with any of us. I understand that this is not always the case, but if at all possible, be sure that you know who you are in Christ before you marry and/or bring children into this world. It is the best way and it is God's way. We must have a foundation of the Word of God within us, in order to teach our children to follow the ways of the Lord and to discover His perfect Will for their lives. The majority of problems we face in this world today originate from doing things our own way, instead of seeking God's Will for our lives. If we follow His guidelines, the Word, then we will see joy in our own lives; therefore, allowing our families to be prosperous, which will ultimately impact the world around us. Our choices not only affect our own lives and the lives of our children, but have the capacity to change the lives of everyone we are connected to. Wow! What a revelation!

So, we see how important it is to *protect* our children's gifts/purpose, even from the womb. I have come to realize through the lives of my own children that God will reveal hints to you about the gifts He has placed within them. From my own experience, I knew very early on that my daughter possessed something very special within her. As we raised her in Christ, her gifts began to develop and she was hearing the voice of the Lord at a very young age. She not only gave her life to Jesus at the age of six, but she also received the Gift of Holy Spirit with the evidence of speaking in tongues at the age of seven. Her growth and maturity in the Word of God was mind blowing! I knew we were teaching her and living as an example before her, but I had no idea what God was doing in and through this little girl in secret. As we are obedient to do our part as parents, He will surely stand over His Word to perform it in the lives of our precious children.

Many parents desire their children to do wonderful things in life and sometimes choose paths for them based upon what the world sees as successful or prominent careers. Because they don't know God for themselves, they don't know to seek Him for what He created in their children. They were not raised in Christ, so they don't know their purpose either. God's ways are absolutely higher than our ways and His thoughts than our thoughts. When we fail to seek Him for what He created in them, we ultimately hinder God's perfect Will for them and they will surely wander through this life aimlessly. It is never too late to find out God's purpose for your life. If you do not know the Lord personally, I humbly ask you to call upon the name of Jesus and seek His love for you. You can read Romans 10:9-10 and ask Him into your heart. Repent of your sins and receive His forgiveness and salvation today.

"… that if you confess with your mouth the Lord Jesus and believe in your heart that God has raised Him from the dead, you will be saved."

We cannot know our gifts outside of God. To realize our life's purpose, we need to know the One that created us; the One who placed that purpose within us! So many in the world today are frustrated, because wealth, status, fame, and notoriety… *nothing* is able to satisfy the deep recesses of our lives, except the love of our Creator. Many refuse to believe in Creation and rather adopt the many other ways in which the world views our existence. I challenge you to seek the possibility that you were, indeed, created by a loving, caring, compassionate, and purposeful Creator, God Himself.

When we receive the revelation in our hearts that we have a loving Creator, then we will search the Word of God as to why He created us and what our purpose is in this life. When we step into this truth, we are destined to fulfill the very purpose for which we were created. This is why we hear of evolution and other philosophies of existence, because Satan surely does not want us to find out our true purpose. His desire is for us to die in our sin, and never experience the fullness of God in the earth. He does not want us to realize our gifts, because they will ultimately *stir up the gifts* of God in others, as well.

The day I found out the purpose for my daughter's life, not only through prophecy, but also by the voice of Holy Spirit, I was challenged. To see the gifts of God flowing through her life at such an early age was mind blowing. The way in which the Lord was using her in the lives of people double and triple her age was undeniable. I stood in awe many days, as grown men wept as she ministered before the Lord. In one service, several men fell to their knees in tears worshiping before their King. Watching this little girl, no more than seven-years-old, fall in love with Jesus was such an inspiration in my own life. The realization hit me that I myself was lost to my purpose, so how could I nurture the gifts on the inside of her? I was thrust into studying the Word of God. I had already been one to read and study the Word and did so consistently, but this was different. Once I made up my mind that I would rely totally upon God for the answers of how to raise this child in His Will, He opened up the Word to me like never before!

"And you will seek Me and find Me, When you search for
Me with all your heart." Jeremiah 29:13

My life and walk with God went to another level. I finally
realized that I had been complacent in the things of God. I was
living the life of a Christian, but not walking in the footsteps of
Jesus. The eyes of my understanding were being enlightened and in
my mind, I had no more excuses to stay dormant in my walk with
the Father. Life began to form within me and doors began to open
to my purpose. God began to reveal, not only through the Word,
but through His servants, what He had purposed for my life and
what He wanted me to do for Him. This is key to understanding
the gifts and calling on your life. When God created purpose in
you, it was not for you, but for others and to bring glory to His
name. Most often when our purpose is revealed to us, the focus
tends to be on us, instead of God. It is the oldest trick in the
enemy's book. He knows it very well, because it was ultimately the
cause of his fall… pride. Our adversary comes to distract us to lead
us away from the very purpose for which we were created.

"Be sober, be vigilant; because the adversary the devil walks
about like a roaring lion, seeking whom he may devour."
1 Peter 5:8

He begins to put the spotlight on you, instead of the One who
gave you purpose. Many times, pride can rise up inside of us if we
do not guard ourselves from the tricks of the enemy. Pride is
probably the single-most cunning spirit one can possess. It takes
you away from God and smothers the true, authentic gifts within
you. In fact, it perverts the gifts and instead of using them to bless
others and bring glory to God, we manipulate them to bring us
profit, fame, and the glory reserved only for the Lord.

We have to remain on the offensive when it comes to
protecting the gifts of God in our lives. Instead of waiting for pride
to manifest in your life, do something about it. Get on your knees

and thank God for who He is in your life and the gifts He has bestowed upon you. Acknowledge that without Him, you can do nothing! As you humbly submit to His plan for your life, He will continue to reveal the many facets of your purpose and manifest the gifts in your life in abundance. Humility pleases God.

> "Therefore humble yourselves under the mighty hand of God, that He may exalt you in due time." 1 Peter 5:6

This is such a crucial scripture when it comes to *protecting* the gifts of God within you. Even though God reveals your purpose to you, it does not mean that the time is now. Many of us move out prematurely, which can hinder and sometimes, taint the precious gifts within us. We can easily become excited that God has shown us how He desires to use us, but what we fail to do is stand still to hear instructions from Holy Spirit. We must trust the process, as we stated earlier, and *protect* what He has revealed to us and allow Him to order our very footsteps.

> "The steps of a good man are ordered by the Lord, And He delights in his way." Psalm 37:23

We have to allow God to lead us through every step of the way, so we do not miss out on His strategic instructions. Since He created the purpose within us, only He knows the steps it will take to reach that purpose. This will take a great deal of patience on our part. Patience is a part of *protecting* the gift. Even though God has shown you the vision; He needs to develop His character within you, as well as the gifts. *Patience* is defined as to persevere or be constant, capable of calmly awaiting an outcome or result, not hasty or impulsive. This word in the Greek is *makrothumeo*, which means *to be long-spirited, forbearing, and patient; patiently endure*. This is what God desires from us, as He continues to reveal more of His plan every day. If we are not willing to be patient, God will not release the fullness of the gifts within us, because He knows it will end in selfishness, not selflessness. Therefore, be still and wait on the Lord!

Another way in which we can *protect* our gifts is to literally keep our mouths closed. Most of us have had at least one experience where God has revealed something to us and we immediately shared it with someone. Again, excitement is usually inevitable. To hear the voice of God speak to us our purpose is overwhelming. We want everyone to know what He has spoken. Please take this advice from me, not everyone is going to be excited about what God is saying to you. Many different situations can arise from this and most are not good responses. Everything we go through in life is a process, which means there is a progression of events that take place before we reach a certain point in our lives. We have to develop a level of hearing from Him and then patiently wait for Him to answer. There are three ways in which we can develop this kind of hearing:

- ❖ Prayer
- ❖ Meditating Upon the Word
- ❖ Receiving the Gift of Holy Spirit

Truly the greatest way to *protect* the gifts on the inside of us is to listen to that "still small voice" within. God wants to speak to His children. He wants to lead us, direct us, guide us, instruct us, and to order our very footsteps. Prayer is the most precious gift God has given to us. To speak to God and to know that He hears us is such a privilege. He desires relationship with His Creation.

> "'Call to Me, and I will answer you, and show you great and mighty things, which you do not know.'" Jeremiah 3:33

He said He will never leave us or forsake us, so develop an intimate prayer life with the Father in Heaven.

And to truly know who He is, and to know His heart, we must know His Word. Jesus is the Word made flesh. He is the embodiment of divinely inspired Scripture. If we want to know Him, we must know the Word. Daily devotion and meditation is imperative in our Christian walk. As we set aside time every day to spend time in the Word of God, He will begin to speak to us through that Word. He desires great things for our lives, but it is attached to the inspired Word of God.

"This Book of the Law shall not depart from your mouth, but you shall meditate in it day and night, that you may observe to do according to all that is written in it. For then you will make your way prosperous, and then you will have good success."
Joshua 1:8

As we read the written Word (logos), He will speak to us through His Spirit (rhema). I heard so much from God through His Word as I began to immerse myself in study and meditation. I grew exponentially in Christ during this season of my life, but something was still missing and I could not figure out what it was? It was not until I was asked if I had received the Gift of Holy Spirit that my hearing His voice clearly began. Holy Spirit enters our life as soon as we receive the gift of salvation through Jesus Christ, but many neglect to tap into His full presence, because they don't understand His role in their lives. As I acknowledged His presence in my life, everything changed. Not only was I hearing His voice for strategic things, but He began to send people into my life that began to speak to and impart the gifts and purpose of God for my life. Holy Spirit is a pertinent part of receiving the gifts of God into our lives, but also the continued hearing needed to carry out His perfect Will for our lives.

We can trust that God will protect the gifts and purpose inside of us, as we draw closer to Him through prayer, meditating upon His Word, and partnering with His Holy Spirit. If you allow yourself to be led by the Spirit of God, many doors will begin to open to you. Again, this takes a lot of patience, humility, and self-sacrifice, but it is more than worth it when you are hearing from God Almighty.

I would sit in my office many days studying the Word of God and giving Holy Spirit reign and rule to reveal the Father's heart to me concerning what He desired for my life. The revelation I was receiving was great. I stood in awe of what I would hear Him say to me, some good and some *not so good*, yet it was all for a greater purpose. I would hear confirmation come from so many sides, the very same thing He had spoken to me in secret. Confirmation is a way in which God solidifies our faith and trust in Him. But just because He sends confirmation does not mean He desires for us to release what He has spoken. Holding our peace in these moments produces a great deal of patience within us, and allows God to trust us with more. Being still does not necessarily mean not doing anything; it simply means to cover and pray over what the Lord has released to you. This allows you great opportunity to strengthen your relationship with Him, because you are totally depending upon His voice, and His voice alone. There is no greater confidant than Holy Spirit Himself! Oh what a true Gift He is!

Another reason not to release information prematurely is because of our adversary, Satan. He would love nothing more than to hinder us from fulfilling God's purpose within us and to steal the very gifts of God in us. Once you release anything into the atmosphere, he immediately begins conjuring up ways to distract you and cause you to abort what God has spoken. Since you have not allowed God to develop your hearing, as well as your patience, the enemy will throw anything he can your way to move you out of your strategic position. 2 Corinthians 2:11 states:

> "… lest Satan should take advantage of us, for we are not ignorant of his devices."

You must *protect* your gifts and purpose at all costs. Do not allow the enemy even a crack to enter in and steal your gifts. We should also use wisdom in whom we share our gifts, purpose, and vision. There are people assigned to walk alongside of you to help support and fulfill the very purpose God has given you. If the person/people you surround yourself with do not make your "baby" jump, if they do not believe in your vision as much as you do and encourage you in it, then you need to re-evaluate your circle of confidants. We see in Scripture how Mary came to see Elizabeth with faith already present in her heart and she encouraged Elizabeth in such a way that the baby in her womb leaped. We know that this was more than mere encouragement; it was the birthing of prophetic destiny!

"And it happened when Elizabeth heard the greeting of Mary, that the babe leaped in her womb, and Elizabeth was filled with the Holy Spirit." Luke 1:41

We must be strategic with whom we allow into our lives when it comes to our purpose. We have to be confident that the people we are sharing intimate details of our journey are assigned by God and not the enemy. Please understand that there should not be many people in this category of confidants. Those God has assigned will be in covenant with you, because not only are they sent to help you, but you are also connected to what God has purposed in their lives. It is a mutual conjoining of agreement, in order to fulfill God's perfect Will. It is reciprocity at its best! This is when you truly know God has sent someone into your life. The fruit will be revealed and it will continue *producing* for the glory of God. We need others to encourage us to stay in the race. It is the "iron sharpening iron," that keeps us focused and prepared for each stage of our journey in Christ. If someone has been allowed to come into your circle to criticize your purpose, then maybe you failed to discern the extent of your relationship. Not saying you have to exude an air of pride or arrogance as if you are too good for them, but maybe you need to re-evaluate the things you can safely share with them concerning your purpose. Simply readjust your relational boundaries and be clear of them. Many times, we simply have not done this in the beginning of relationships; therefore, leaving the door wide open for people to be very vocal when it comes to what God has called us to do. By setting these boundaries in the beginning, we can curb much of these *hiccups* along the way. God is calling us to *protect* the gifts within and one aspect of that is relationship.

This leads to the covering aspect of *protecting your gift*. The vision God has placed within you is supported wholly by the Word of God. The gift, or purpose, in you must line up with His Word and be led by Holy Spirit. God does not merely create a person; He creates Purpose! We must cover our gift with the Word. Again, how can we know our purpose if we do not know the One who created it within us? Get to know your Father and find out what He has purposed for your life. Embrace Holy Spirit within, so you are able to hear clearly what He is saying to you. The enemy would love nothing more than to confuse and distract you in your hearing. This is a very crucial step, because it will save you from making many mistakes when it comes to knowing who you are hearing from. Be filled with Holy Spirit and seek His infilling daily, so you are able to tap into Heaven's mind for your life. In simply reading the Word of God, we are able to grasp some good concepts that we can apply to our everyday lives, but God desires us to know Him on a deeper level; intimately through the ministry of Holy Spirit. What Holy Spirit provides the believer in Christ is something that cannot be obtained by merely reading the Word of God.

"… who also made us sufficient as ministers of the new covenant, not of the letter but of the Spirit; for the letter kills, but the Spirit gives life." 2 Corinthians 3:6

Holy Spirit illuminates, brings life and revelation to, the written Word of God. He provides insight into the mysteries of God that normally would not be revealed through natural understanding. Many Christians remain frustrated, because they have settled for a mediocre relationship with God, instead of a Spirit-filled, life-giving daily interaction with Holy Spirit. Seek greater from the Father and He will open up new dimensions to you.

If you were like me, I would read a scripture over and over again, not really understanding how it was supposed to apply to my life. It was not until I received the infilling of Holy Spirit that the Word began to truly open up to me. I was ignorant and immature in the things of the Spirit. I had prayed fervently for God to reveal Himself to me for years. I was a student of the Word, but something crucial was missing from my life as a follower of Jesus Christ. I did not know how to access the power of God, and did not know He was another Gift God wanted me to receive. I had to recognize His ministry in my life and find out what His purpose was before I was able to access mine. In the writing of my book *Holy Spirit*[3] , which culminated over a period of four to five years, God submerged me into a place where I desperately sought His voice in my life. I was in a place of deep brokenness, initiated by the Lord, to seek Him on levels I had never before experienced. It was during this time that I was tutored by Holy Spirit, Himself. He was imparting His presence within me and allowing me to learn how to cover the precious gifts of God.

Jesus had to physically die in the earth realm for Holy Spirit to be released. He did not pour out His Spirit for us to sit back and wonder what lies ahead for our lives. He desires us to receive this precious, free Gift and allow Him to lead us by the prompting of His Spirit, or our inner witness. Many, even in the church today, call it their conscious, but it is, in fact, Holy Spirit within. If you are

---

[3] *Holy Spirit: The Promised Left For the Believer.* Hunter, Deborah G. Hunter Heart Publishing/Hunter Entertainment Network. Colorado Springs, Colorado, 2016.

a born-again believer in Jesus Christ, you invited Holy Spirit to live within you. You may not have known the full assignment of Holy Spirit, but He is, indeed, available to you. You must allow Him the opportunity to fulfill His assignment in your life. Let Him lead, guide, direct, and instruct you in *protecting* and covering what is on the inside of you. Being able to hear clearly from Holy Spirit will be one of the greatest gifts you will ever receive.

As you cover your gifts and purpose with the Word and seek the voice of God concerning His purpose, He will reveal His thoughts and intent concerning you and your place in the Kingdom! I encourage you to stand strong and trust in the Lord that He will bring your gifts and purpose full-term if you allow the process to take place in your life. Believe in your heart that He is well able to finish the good work that He started within you before you were even formed in your mother's womb. Become determined that you will *protect* the gifts at all costs and that you will see it through until the end. *Stir Up the Gift*!

5

Profiting from the Gift

Most people, at one time or another, have desired to profit from certain abilities, talents, or gifting. We feel because we have either attended school to obtain a degree, or gained valuable life experience in a certain area that we have the "right" to produce financially from it. This is not in debate whatsoever, but when it comes to the gifts and purpose of the Kingdom, God needs us to see another dimension of *profiting*. The word *profit* is defined as an advantageous gain or return; benefit. The Hebrew word is *ya'al*, which means *to ascend, to be valuable, useful, or profitable*. We clearly see the difference between the world's view of profitability and God's ultimate plan and purpose for His people. God desires for His people to be useful to and for His Kingdom. We are valuable to the furtherance of His Will in the earth realm, not to merely benefit us, but to be a benefit to others.

"But seek first the Kingdom of God and His righteousness, and all those things shall be added to you." Matthew 6:33

Many faith and prosperity teachings twist this scripture around and teach more upon the "things" we receive from God, instead of being a tool in the hand of God in the building His Kingdom. The error in this kind of teaching paves the way for pride, arrogance, greed, and entitlement. The wisdom of God is absolutely clear in this scripture… *seek first the Kingdom of God and His righteousness!* The Kingdom reveals to us that we are granted *citizenship*; righteousness signifies the *access* given to us by God. In understanding these two very crucial aspects, we should never worry about, or seek out, material things from the Lord. He will add what is needed to and for our daily lives. When we refuse to teach this correctly, we open the door for great deception in our lives.

As we saw previously, some feel they have the right to profit how they see fit, or how they feel they deserve to be compensated, yes, even from God. But the Word says to seek His *righteousness*, or right-standing, alignment. His right-standing/alignment is His character, His ways, and His Will. If we are not in right-standing/alignment with God, nothing we receive in this life will be *profitable* for His Kingdom, but merely a means of bringing us further away from His plan and purpose. We understand the enemy's agenda in our lives is to keep the focus on ourselves and what we can *get* from God, instead of being a vessel God is able to use for the glory of His Kingdom. Again, we are created with a purpose, and that purpose is attached to a larger vision. Many see Scripture as an absolute, meaning it will automatically come to pass in my life if I am a follower of Jesus Christ. This is not scriptural and neither is it expedient in the long run of our lives. There is always a part A and part B in every scripture. If part A is not fulfilled, then part B will not be manifested in our lives, which signifies the *profiting* in the Word of God. Let's look at an example:

"If you abide in Me, and My words abide in you, you will ask what you desire, and it shall be done for you. By this My Father is glorified, that you bear much fruit; so you will be My disciples." John 15:7-8

This scripture is conditional. Jesus says, "*If* you abide in Me and My words abide in you…" Many believe they can live any way they desire and simply because they *identify* themselves as a Christian,

God will give them whatever they ask. This is error and the topic for much false teaching in the church today. Why would God give us what we ask, or desire, if our will is not lined up with His? He knows very well it will lead to our destruction. If what we ask for does not line up with His Word, His Will, then it is not *of* Him. And as we see, God is glorified when we *profit*, or bear fruit, His way. It is only here where we can be identified as authentic disciples of the Kingdom.

We know that God is the giver of good things, but we must understand that not everything *good* is *God*. Our job is to figure out, through the leading of Holy Spirit, what is of Him and what is not. This is called *discernment*. Discernment is defined as the act or process of exhibiting keen insight and good judgment. The Hebrew word is *yada*, which means *to know, acknowledge, be acquainted with, be aware, or have understanding*. Now to have good judgment is one thing, but to have understanding is what we should desire from the Lord. In the Hebrew definition, it shows us that we are not to lean to our own knowledge, but to be aware of, or acknowledge, that there is a higher insight we need to seek, not our own. When it comes to *profiting* from the gifts God has endowed upon us, we should view it from Scripture, not the world.

"Wisdom is the principle thing; therefore get wisdom. And in all your getting, get understanding." Proverbs 4:7

You can have two men at a car dealership seeking to purchase a new vehicle. One man has been informed by the sales associate of all the *perks* that come with his new purchase. Because it sounds like a great deal, he immediately decides he will buy the car. The second man has also been told of all he will receive extra from making this purchase, but instead of jumping right away at the offer because it *sounds good*, tells the associate that he will think about it (pray about it) and will get back with him. The second gentleman most assuredly made the wise decision, because again, not everything that looks or sounds good is necessarily the right thing to do. Too many Believers in Christ make rash decisions, without seeking Holy Spirit if this is God's Will for their lives. Instead of being led by the Spirit, they are guided by their flesh.

When God desires for us to be *profitable*, He is looking at how the gift will benefit the Kingdom of God here on earth, and yes, ultimately, for eternity. The gift God has given you is not for you, but for others. He will allow your will to be conformed to His, so you can partner with Him in the earth realm.

"And be not conformed to this world: but be ye transformed by the renewing of your mind, that ye may prove what is that good, and acceptable, and perfect, will of God." Romans 12:2

Our minds must be transformed, in order to be used by God to further His Will. It is very easy to be deceived by the enemy into thinking God does not want us blessed. This is one of the greatest lies of the devil. But an even greater one is making us believe that prosperity is God's number one priority for our lives. This, again, is false teaching. The Word says in 3 John 2 that he prayed that Gaius, an elder, may prosper in all things and be in good health, even as his soul prospers. Again, one of the most twisted scriptures in the Bible by faith and prosperity teaching! John is commending Gaius for the truth that is in him. Because he walked in truth, other Believers were able to see his witness and example, and seek to walk in that same truth. He was *profitable* for the Kingdom. John was not stating that he prayed for Gaius to be "rich" or that it was God's Will for him to be financially prosperous. He was speaking of the blessing of God following Gaius, the kind of prosperity that could not be lost or taken away.

The word *prosperity* means the state of being prosperous, success, profitability, wealth, opulence, luxury, or the good life; plenty, comfort, fortune, security, or well-being. This word in Hebrew, according to 3 John 2, is *tselach*, meaning *to advance, succeed in, accomplish, or carry out.* John was commending Gaius for the work of Christ in his heart; the Christ-inhabited soul. The truly prosperous soul is one that walks in Spirit and in Truth. It is not self-seeking, but desires to do the Will of God, to the glory of God. Gaius was being *rewarded* for his faithfulness in living out the Gospel. He, and I am sure even his fellow brothers and sisters in the Lord, were not seeking to *profit* financially from the Gospel, but to be true examples of Jesus Christ, and John recognized this with his heartfelt prayer for this disciple. This is the true heart of this short, but profound, letter from John. And if we read down further in 3 John, we see this expounded upon even greater.

"Beloved, you do faithfully whatever you do for the brethren and for strangers, who have borne witness of your love before the church. If you send them forward on their journey in a manner worthy of God, you will do well, because they went forth for His name's sake, taking *nothing* from the Gentiles. We therefore ought to receive such, that we may become fellow workers for the truth." 3 John 5-8 (emphasis)

Now, Gaius may have very well sent the brethren with provision for their journey, and may have blessed even strangers monetarily, but the most important lesson of this book is the imperishable traits of a Christ-centered life. Many choose to *read into* these verses, or *manipulate them*, and come to the conclusion that these are grounds for reaping financially for faithfulness. It is so much more than that; Gaius' life was *profitable* for the Kingdom of God! Others' lives were transformed by this living epistle. His life was *read* by men, and in turn, their lives were forever changed by this faithful servant.

So many in the Body of Christ are not being taught to lay down their lives for the Gospel. Instead, they are being encouraged to get all they can get from God. Once we give our lives freely to the Lord, we are no longer our own. We have to understand that we have *traded* our lives for His Will. We have to come in agreement with His plan and purpose for our lives, and to be used by

Almighty God as He sees fit. Whatever wants and desires we had before surrendering our lives to God must be submitted to His Word, His Will. And we must be okay with giving up anything that will hinder His perfect plan from coming to pass in our lives.

I look back at my life to several instances in my childhood where I was confronted with life and death circumstances. I thought then that it was my destiny to become a nurse, but as I look back, I see it was an opportunity to witness the love of Jesus Christ. One night, I was at my sister's house and we were outside with some friends. We saw two little girls running across the street in their pajamas. I approached them to make sure they were okay, because they were crying and it was completely dark outside. Suddenly, their mother came out and approached me with blood all over her nightgown. I asked her what happened and she said her husband was beating her and she stabbed him with a kitchen knife. I was about sixteen-years-old at this time, but instinctively, I ran into the house to see if he was still alive. This man's entire mid-section was cut into and his intestines were literally hanging out of him. Something inside of me told me to push them back inside of him and hold them there to put pressure to stop the bleeding, until the ambulance came. I grabbed a towel and did exactly that.

I remember speaking to him and asking him if there was anything he wanted to say and he simply said, "I'm sorry." At the time, I did not know what he was saying sorry for. Maybe he was saying he was sorry for what he had done to his wife and children, or maybe all of the things that had led to his abusiveness? Maybe he was, at that moment of knowing he was going to die, asking God to forgive him? I did not know to witness Jesus to this man at that time, and that God would forgive him if he just asked Him into his heart right there. But I now understand that God used me in this moment in time to *be* the love of Christ in this man's dying moments. I held his hand and told him that he did not have to die with this guilt upon his life. I told him he would not die alone… at sixteen- years-old! I had been saved at twelve, but my life during that four year period was not spent in the church, or learning anything about how to live for Christ. In fact, two years earlier, I had tried to take my own life! What was God doing here? I was literally the last face this man saw before he passed away. As I look back, I remember sensing something other than myself and this man in the room with us. I now know the presence of God was right there with us, leading this man to repentance and into the presence of God Almighty.

Another instance I remember was when I was about nineteen-years-old. A friend of mine wrecked his truck in our front yard. He was speeding around a sharp curve right before our house, and hit the ditch and went airborne over our fence. He was thrown from the truck and it landed on top of him. I had been driving home from work and noticed the fence broken and a truck in our front yard. I immediately stopped my car and got out and jumped over the fence. I ran to the truck and saw him pinned underneath. I could see his arm hanging out and again, instinctively, I grabbed his hand and began talking with him, until the paramedics came. I reminded him that he was not alone, and not to be afraid. I did not know, at the time, that this was a schoolmate of mine, until near the end when the paramedics and police were asking if I knew who this was. I stood there for a minute saying, "This truck looks familiar." I could not see the boy's face; I could only see his arm and hand. Instantly, I knew who it was. I now know Holy Spirit was the One that had revealed this to me. His girlfriend lived down the street from us, so I rode with the police to her house to break the news to her that he was deceased. I remember sitting there holding her and encouraging this young girl that God would comfort her.

Again, I believe I was the last voice this boy heard before he died. If I had been in the proper *position* to witness Jesus to him, this could have been the deciding factor of his salvation. For so long, we are told that there is a *formula* to accepting Jesus into our lives. I do believe that if we confess with our mouths the Lord

Jesus and believe in our hearts that God has raised Him from the dead that we will be saved. But one thing I have learned over my saved life is that the presence of God in extenuating circumstances is very real and very present. Why did God place me in these particular situations? Why did I feel His love so strong in my heart to give to these men in their last moments of life? I may not ever know, but He does. I now know God was positioning me for the call of God upon my life.

From as far back as I can remember, I wanted to be a nurse. I attended several nursing programs to further my education, but it never materialized. I had a full scholarship and plane tickets in my hand to attend Penn State University's Nursing program, but God said not to accept it. Once I gave my life back to Christ, this was no longer a desire for me, per say, in the physical realm, but became more of a spiritual desire. Don't get me wrong, being a nurse is absolutely an admirable career and a necessary profession in this world, but for me, God closed every door in my life in this area. My desire began to move towards helping people spiritually through the Word of God and my life experiences. He changed my desires, as I began to renew my mind through His Word. He caused my desires to line up with His perfect Will for my life. And let me tell you, I have never felt more like a *nurse* in my life! God has used me tremendously in the inner healing and spiritual transformation of people's lives, and it is the most rewarding gift I could have ever received.

Our lives are no longer our own and when we surrender to God's calling upon our lives, He can and will do the miraculous through us. When God knows we are sold out, surrendered, and submitted to His Will and that nothing can turn us away from it, He causes us to *profit* greatly. He provides us with all we need to accomplish His plan and purposes in the earth, not only in our own lives, but in the lives of others, as well. The *profiting* of the Lord is for the furthering of the Kingdom of God *in* and *through* you. Gaius' faithfulness to the purpose in his life gave way for God to bless every area of his life, including his health, possibly long life to continue spreading the Gospel. It was not because he *deserved* it, but because he was faithful. There was no motive in Gaius other than to serve the Lord and His people. He didn't demand God bless him, because of his obedience. It is our duty to be obedient to God, even if He *never* rewards us here on this earth. But we see that God used John to strengthen and encourage Gaius along his journey through this prayer. When we begin to feel we deserve things from God, then we have stepped out of His Will, because we deserve *nothing* but judgment from Him! It is only by His grace and mercy that we are saved and only because of His plan and purposes that we are still here, able to witness of His goodness.

"… who saved us and called us with a holy calling, not according to our own works, but according to His own purpose and grace which was given to us in Christ Jesus before time began." 2 Timothy 1:9

There it goes again, God created in us purpose before time began, so we will never *profit* from the gifts and purpose within us, unless we have lined back up with the original intent and purposes of God Almighty. Have you heard of fortune-tellers or astrologers that claim when the moons have lined up in a specific order that prosperity will come into your life? We know that this is not of God, and a form of great deception, but take this concept and apply it to God's purpose for your life. We are created with purpose before we are born into this world. We are raised by our parents who instill their values and traditions within us that have been passed down throughout the generations. We grow older and meet many different people along the way who share their views of life with us and some may very well witness the love of Jesus Christ to us. You receive the witness to be true inside of you and choose to live for Christ. You were never before seeing change in your life, until you gave your life over to Jesus. You have now *stepped back into* the reason, or purpose, for which you were created. Every life experience you have gone through, led you *back* to God's intended plan for your life. God used these seasons of your life to *line you up* with His perfect Will for your life.

Now that your purpose is manifesting, you are being transformed daily into His image. The more we become like Him, the more He can trust us to carry out His Will, and the more He will release to fulfill His purposes through us. This is the kind of *profiting* we should be seeing in our walk with the Lord. Don't be deceived into thinking it is all about you, and lose your position in the Kingdom of God.

> "There is a way that seems right to a man, but its end is the way of death." Proverbs 14:12

The way of the Cross is not a selfish road; it is the most selfless act of love we can ever give back to our Lord who gave Himself for us. It is going the extra mile for God to release His favor upon your life and for His glory to be revealed through you. We are called to let our light shine that others may see our good works and glorify our Father in Heaven. Our lives should cause others to want Him in their lives. This is the *profiting* of the Gospel in our lives. The fruit is not merely temporal, it is eternal in nature. Our fruit should be producing even more fruit in the lives of those we come into contact with every day.

Guard the gifts and purpose within you no matter what it looks like in the natural. You may fail to see the *profit* you are producing in the Kingdom right away. This is one way in which Satan tries to deceive us, by distraction. He may tell you, "It is not worth it," "All of this Christian stuff is too much work," "I can get what I want quicker than this," or "It just doesn't take all of that" and that there are other ways in which we can obtain the things we desire. We must understand how our adversary thinks and moves to get us out of position. Anytime we try to bypass the process of preparation, the way of God, for the "short-cut," we better be ready to meet Satan right on that road. This is his way. He doesn't want to see you transformed by the process. He hates to see God's character formed within people. God encourages us to remain patient, long-suffering, and to wait upon the Lord; to stand strong and be of good courage; endure patiently, abound in faith, and possess self-control. I believe God gives us these attributes to *set us apart* from the world, to reveal Himself through us to a blinded world. If we cannot see these characteristics being displayed in our lives, then must ask ourselves if we have fallen out of His Will.

Many Believers throughout history have given up on the race, because it was taking too long for them. They may have felt God was punishing them or that maybe He was simply *not real*, because they were not seeing the blessing of God upon their lives. Again, if you have given your life to Christ, you are no longer your own. If you are not seeking the Father and being obedient and waiting patiently on Him, you will not see the *profit* that can only come to *"those who love the Lord and are called according to His Purpose."* Many of us come to God thinking it will be an easy walk, but find out quickly that it is absolutely not! It does take work, but not the kind of work we think it should be. We work by studying and meditating upon the Scriptures to get to know Him better. When we do this consistently, He gives us His *peace that surpasses all of our understanding.* When we begin to know who He is through His Word, we find it easier to serve Him in our families, in our workplace, and in our local places of worship.

To truly *profit* in our gifts and calling, our purpose, it takes much discipline. We have to make this a lifestyle, not just a mere *quick fix* when we find ourselves in trouble and need a Word from the Lord. We have to be set in position to hear clearly from God and this comes by surrounding ourselves with Believers of like faith. As we learned in the last chapter, we *protect* our gifts and purpose by walking alongside God-appointed people. Spiritual mentors are very crucial in the development of our gifts and calling.

"Finally then brethren, we urge and exhort in the Lord Jesus
that you should abound more and more, just as you received
from us how you ought to walk and to please God."
1 Thessalonians 4:1

Many believe they don't need anyone to carry out God's plan
for their lives. This, too, is deception. God did not call us to live
this life in isolation, separated from others that can sharpen us in
the Lord. This is a sign of rebellion. God has given us shepherds
after His own heart that will feed us with knowledge and
understanding (Jeremiah 3:15). These authentic gifts are so very
precious and needed in our lives. I understand that many pastors
have been deceived and are deceiving; this does not mean that it
wasn't, and still is, very vital to our growth in Christ and the
fulfillment of our calling in the earth.

"And if you have not been found faithful in what is another
man's, who will give you what is your own?" Luke 16:12

Please know that God will never release something to you that
is not connected to someone else's vision. Each vision is connected
to the larger vision of establishing the Kingdom of God in the
earth realm. No one in the Body of Christ is free of influence from
another person in Christ. If you are, then you are definitely not
operating as a part of the Body of Christ or according to Scripture.
And you are most likely not *profiting* from the Lord, but from Satan.

"From whom the whole body fitly joined together and
compacted by that which every joint supplieth, according to the
effectual working in the measure of every part, maketh increase
of the body unto the edifying of itself in love." Ephesians 4:6

God's desire is that we be *fitly joined together*, similar to that of a
puzzle; whereas, if one piece is missing, the entire puzzle is useless
and good for nothing. Also like a body where limbs are missing,
causing the entire body not to function properly as it was created.

We need one another to accomplish His Will for our lives. God will also surround us with mentors and confidants that will not only speak into our lives, but who can also be an ear to hear when we need them. Your life is strategically connected *to* and *with* other Believers… embrace those relationships. You need them and they need you!

We must also stop assuming what it is that God wants *for us* and read His Word where He gives us all He will ever desire *from us*, so He can give *to us* what we are seeking of Him. This is an intimate relationship between Creator and creation, God and friend, Father and son. You have to give in order to receive. It takes us obeying His commandments in order to *profit* in the way of Scripture. We make our lives more difficult than it has to be, because we refuse to obey His voice at all times. We conveniently pick and choose which scriptures we want to abide by, and reject the others that have the potential to transform our old man into the new. We skip the parts that challenge us to live for Christ and to develop His character within us. Instead, we seek *quick fixes* to our problems and refuse to slow down in order to hear clearly what the Spirit of God is saying to us.

You should now have a better understanding that the gift, purpose, and calling on your life is for the furthering of His Kingdom and not the furthering of your own agendas. Everything we do now, as a follower of Christ, should be for His glory and His purpose; to please Him. We spoke earlier of the *favor* of God and how it has been misconstrued for so long. Many have false perceptions of what God's intent for this word truly means. *Favor* is defined as something done out of good will; a kind act; excessive kindness or unfair partiality; preferential treatment. This word in Greek is *charis*, which means *graciousness, the divine influence upon the heart, acceptable, benefit, favour, gift, grace, joy, liberality, pleasure, or thanks.* God's *favor* is not sent for our benefit, but for His. We are simply conduits that house His *favor* so that His purposes are fulfilled in the earth. Favor is also mentioned as the unmerited grace of God.

This means we do nothing in order to receive it, but it is simply because of His goodness that He allows us to obtain His *favor*. Favor is God *divinely influencing* people's hearts and situations through us for His glory.

God desires His children to walk and operate in *His favor* in this earth, so unbelievers will see us and ask, "How?" This is the opportunity for God to receive the glory due His name. As Believers in Christ Jesus, we should never desire anything that will not reveal His glory in our lives. What I mean by this is, for example, if you desire a new car and the dealer is offering a huge rebate, extra money off for military members, add-ons at no extra cost, and even willing to give you his employee discount, do you consider this as God's favor? It can be classified as a *good deal*, but not the *favor of God*. You can walk into a real estate deal expecting to pay $500,000 for a brand new home, and walk out paying only $250,000. This may be a blessing from God, but this, too, is not the meaning of the *favor of God*. I have found in over 20+ years of walking with God that the favor upon our lives is to bring the knowledge of Him into others' lives. People, souls, are attached to God releasing His *favor* upon you. Don't be so naïve to think mere *things* are the result of the *favor of God*. It is not the corruptible that stands the test of time, it is the incorruptible; the things of eternal value.

God desires us to be a light in the midst of this dark world. People need what we possess. They, deep down, are hungering and thirsting for something that will satisfy the longing of their souls. No man, no woman, no money, no homes, no cars, no clothes, no business, no status, no fame, no wealth, and no fans can fill the void that only God Himself can occupy! Many are waking up to this reality; some died in it. What you have on the inside of you, the Greater One living within, is more precious than gold; more valuable than rubies. We must make up in our minds that *this* is what is most important and refuse to *profit* in the ways of the world. We should refuse to accept anything that does not bring glory to the Father. We should challenge ourselves in *every* situation to find out how it can bring others into the saving knowledge and love of Jesus Christ.

As I found out that I would actually write my first book, I had several other people in my church that had written books. Several had already published and led me to the companies they were working with on their books. I began to write my book and stayed in touch with these companies during the process. They offered wonderful advice and encouragement, as I rounded each turn. I thought I had narrowed it down to the publisher I would choose to go with, but Holy Spirit led me in a different direction. He told me that I would self-publish, which consisted of me doing *everything* a publisher would do for me. I explained this to the publisher, and I was attacked saying I wasted their time! What an experience, but there was no doubt in my mind this was where God was leading me.

I was nervous, at first, but the peace of God blanketed me when I heard Holy Spirit say, "What do you desire more, notoriety and wealth, or the glory of God, *favor*, to be released in your life?" This was absolutely sobering for me and moved me into a new level of faith and trust in God. I knew, at that moment, I did not need worldwide exposure from a well-known publisher, because God had my back; He would make Himself my publisher! Glory to God! He told me to write to the praise of His glory and not to worry about how anything was going to get done, because it was in His hands. Little did I know then that this would be the beginning of a ministry of writing that has spanned almost twenty years? It has proven to be the training, equipping, and empowering of Holy Spirit Himself as I placed pen to paper every morning (now finger to keys, smile). God has led me by His Spirit in every book that I have written, and I can plainly see how each book written, and the sequence in which they were released, was truly the *divinely inspired* hand of God.

In my obedience to keep writing, He would open the door for my own publishing company. It was neither a desire nor a want of mine, but He would place the desire within me to help others get their message, His story in their lives, out to the world. Now, six personal books later, thousands of books sold, over fifty books published by our authors, with tens of thousands printed and sold, and countless lives touched and transformed by the Word of God and the power of testimony, I have seen a *glimpse* of what the Lord desires from our gifts and our purpose. It took fifteen years for me to see any real financial profit from my own personal books, but I remained faithful and continued to write what the Lord was telling me to write. I did not get discouraged or give up. I understood that lives were being touched by the words I wrote. It may not have been tens of thousands then, but that was not God's plan. He wanted to see if one life was worth the fifteen years of committed writing. He was putting me to the test to solidify His promise within me and the extension through this publishing company. I can say I passed this test, but it took me surrendering and submitting my will to His. The authentic *profiting* through the gifts, purpose, and calling on my life had to be ingrained within me. I had to see the true and lasting benefits and make them my priority.

We do not need what the world has to offer us, which is really nothing in comparison to what our Almighty Father has for us. It really cannot be compared. We must become determined that because we are His sons, He will provide us with everything we need in order to fulfill our purpose, our calling, our assignment in the earth. And we must be persuaded that no devil in hell can offer us anything in its place. We have to purpose in our hearts to live for Him and allow our lives to glorify Him. Do not compromise the eternal for the temporal.

"Thus says the Lord, your Redeemer, The Holy One of Israel: 'I am the Lord your God, Who teaches you to profit, Who leads you by the way you should go." Isaiah 48:17

There is no real *profit* without perseverance. There is no real *profit* without persecution. There is no real *profit* without purpose. You are profitable for the Kingdom of God! Allow God to *Stir up the Gift* within you for His glory!

6

The Promise of the Gift

Throughout our lives, we go through many different changes, or stages, from our family life to our careers. There will always be a progression of events that take place in our lives, in order to walk out the fullness of God. We may want to remain hidden and live quiet, peaceful lives in seclusion, but as a child of God, we simply cannot. The Spirit of God within us will not let us. Some children wish they could stay little forever. They don't want to grow up, because they understand things will change. With age come responsibilities and accountability. Everything changes! We have to eventually grow up and become adults, but more importantly, we have to develop in maturity, in order to walk in the *promise* of God for our lives. His desire is for His children to grow and mature, so we can become effective witnesses in the earth. We are to progress from children into sons of God and for this to happen, each level we saw previously is necessary. Our lives are not merely a coincidence or a happenstance. Our Father knew everything that would ever happen in our lives; therefore, using each relationship, situation, and circumstance to draw us closer towards our gifts, purpose, calling, and assignment… closer to His manifested presence in our lives.

I know it is not easily understood, or comprehended, "If God knew what our lives would entail, why would He allow such horrible things to happen to us?" I do not claim to know everything concerning God or what He is doing in my life or yours, nor do I desire to know it all. What I do know is that He has a *promise* for my life and yours and everything: past, present, and future, is needed for what He created in us to be made manifest in the earth. My life has been a very difficult one, but as I look back, I do not regret anything, because it has made me the woman I am today. It has revealed His great love, mercy, grace, and yes, His glory in my life. I am who I am today, because of everything I have experienced in my life.

Once we come into the full knowledge of God's Will for our lives, we can look back at each stage we had to go through and see Him in it and understand it better. God does not reveal our full purpose completely to us instantly, because He knows we will most likely not go through the necessary process of refining. When we finally see a target we spent years trying to reach, we tend not to work as hard to obtain it, because we feel it is now within our reach. We must allow the process to prepare us for the *promise*, so we do not miss all that takes place in between. Each new day in Christ brings us closer to Him, to a new level of faith in Him, and to a new aspect of His purpose in our lives. Many of us desire for God to release it all to us, to just pour it all out, but He knows we cannot handle it all at once. Remember, character must be formed within us to carry the weight of the Gospel in our lives. Too much, too soon, causes huge distractions in our lives and will surely take us away from our Lord. Many throw themselves into Bible College, seminary, and theological institutions in order to obtain degrees and titles, thinking they know so much about God, yet know so little. I am not discounting Biblical education, I, too, have it, but what I am saying is nothing can replace the intimate places God desires to take us through, in order to reach the *promise* He has for our lives. I thought I knew Him well, but found out that I didn't really know Him at all. His thoughts are higher than our thoughts and His ways higher than our ways. God's litmus test is our willingness to go through His process… His way, His timing, and for His glory! We must have faith in Him that He knows what is absolutely best for us. We must be in right-standing, or aligned, with His Will to prosper in the gifts and calling of God.

> "For in it the righteousness of God is revealed from faith to faith; as it is written: 'The just shall live by faith.'" Romans 1:17

My desire to know the Father multiplied greatly through the trials I have experienced over my lifetime. I have come to a place where I no longer have to see it to believe it. I have a better understanding of what it means to follow Christ, and my life has changed drastically from twenty years ago. Faith is the key to walking in the Will of God. Through my experiences, my faith has grown exponentially. *Faith* is defined as confidence or trust in a person or thing, belief in God or in teachings of religion or belief that is based on proof. This word in Greek is *pistis*, which means *persuasion, credence, conviction, reliance, constancy, assurance, belief, or faith.* Do you see the drastic difference between the world's views of faith and how we, as followers of Christ, are supposed to be persuaded of His plan and promise for our lives. There is the word *persuaded* again. You cannot walk in the *promise* of God for your life if you are not fully persuaded, in faith, of His plan for your life. You must remain persuaded, regardless of what it looks like, feels like, and no matter what circumstances you find yourself in. This does not change His *promise* for your life; it has no bearing whatsoever on God's timetable. Stay in faith!

> "But without faith it is impossible to please Him, for he who comes to God must believe that He is, and that He is a rewarder of those who diligently seek Him." Hebrews 11:6

We have to believe Him if we want to move forward in His Will. Our problem is doubting when we do not see things manifesting quickly enough. We are our worst enemy sometimes, because we refuse to believe what God has spoken over our lives. Even Satan believes it and this is his entire reason for planting worry and doubt in our hearts. He does not want us to get revelation concerning the gifts and calling on our lives. God's Word is settled in Heaven concerning your life, come into agreement with it today. His *promises* are true!

"For all the promises of God in Him are Yes, and in Him Amen, to the glory of God through us." 2 Corinthians 1:20

You can have peace in your life knowing that God's *promises* are faithful and He will stand over His Word to perform it in your life. You can stand boldly in the face of the enemy by walking out the Will of God for your life. When we finally have the courage and faith to believe this, we can release those faith killers in our lives, including worry, doubt, unforgiveness, anxiety, stress, impatience, bitterness, resentment, and many others. We have to know who we are and whose we are, in order to walk in the *promises* of God. In my book *Breaking the Eve Mentality*[4], we saw how Eve fell, because she failed to recognize who she was and whose she was. She failed to usurp the authority God had given to her and Adam over all the creatures of the earth.

When we fail to hold our strategic positions in the earth that God has ordained over our lives, we hand it over to the enemy. God was angry when He knew what Adam and Eve had done. He was disappointed by the fact they chose to believe a cunning serpent, instead of a loving Creator. I can only imagine how He felt when they handed over the *promises* of God for the devil's lies. Their fellowship with God was broken and their place in the Garden was compromised. Praise God He had a back-up plan! He has given us His Only Son, Jesus Christ, and no matter how many times we fall short, we can get back up again and continue on our

---

[4] *Breaking the Eve Mentality.* Hunter, Deborah G. Hunter Heart Publishing, Colorado Springs, Colorado. Originally published 2005/Revised 2010.

journey towards His *promise* in and over our lives. Don't give up and don't allow the enemy to kill, steal, and destroy His plan for your life.

Walking with the Lord is such a precious privilege. He walked alongside Adam and Eve in the Garden in unbroken fellowship, and He desires the same for you and me. Many choose to run ahead of Him and therefore miss the *promises* of God. We cannot separate Him from the very gifts, purpose, and calling on our lives. The word "walk" in Greek is *yalak*, which means *to walk, carry, bear, grow, lead, let down, march, or prosper.* It must be a partnership between you and the Lord to carry out His Will in the earth. Too many today are preaching this easy Christianity. They erroneously claim God wants to give us everything we ask for and that He wants us to always be happy. This cannot be furthest from the truth! Yes, God loves us, but He strengthens us through adversity. His character is formed in our lives through the process. Jesus' walk with God was the single-most painful walk anyone has ever, or will, experience in this world. But it led Him to His *Promise*. We must become weak, so God can show Himself strong in and through us. You will have to bear some things in your life before entering into the *promises* of God. His glory is being revealed through every test, trial, and adversity you face. Jesus bore the very weight of the world on His shoulders on His way to the *Promise*.

All too often, we hear of Christians boasting of their years of being saved and going to church. Many start out with good intentions, and do honorable things, but totally miss the *promises* of God for their lives here on the earth. The very gifts, calling, and assignment He created within them goes untapped, because of tradition or religion. The most devastating thing I have seen over the past twenty years is church pews filled with unrecognized gifts. Either our shepherds are not able to discern them, or they are outright stifling the very gifts God has endowed upon His precious children. But we, as believers, have a responsibility to seek God for them and to ask Him to stir them up within us. But please understand that as you begin to seek them, great resistance will come from our enemy. This walk is not an easy one and honestly, it was never intended to be, Biblically. There are scriptures upon scriptures that reveal what the true, authentic Believer will face, as we lay down our lives for the cause of Christ. I have come to experience many great testings in my walk with God, but each has produced a greater faith and trust in the Lord. If you are a Believer in Christ Jesus and you have not had to endure some type of testing or adversity, then you need to ask yourself if you are truly in the Will of God for your life.

"Knowing that the testing of your faith produces patience."
James 1:3

This testing it not merely a onetime occurrence, but an ongoing process that continues to produce fruit in our lives. The Word says we will go from "faith to faith, and glory to glory"... a process! If we desire to walk in the *promises* of God for our lives, we are going to have to wait on Him. We have to go through the process of refining from God through each and every test He desires for us, in order to obtain the *promise*. We should stay clear of constant complaining as we wait patiently upon the Lord. This can cause a great delay in receiving His promises, because our attitude gets in the way. We must understand that our attitude will determine our altitude. Don't allow the lack of humility to keep you in a "wilderness" season longer than you have to be there. Did we hear our Lord complain through His process on the way to His *Promise*? I am sure He did not enjoy one bit of it, but His statement in the Garden of Gethsemane reveals the heart of God in relation to patience, "Nevertheless, not My will, but Your will be done." My God! What an example! He patiently endured all, because He was focused on the *Promise*.

Abraham, too, had to believe and receive what God had spoken to him and walk through the process of preparation, on his way to the *Promise*.

"For when God made a promise to Abraham, because He could swear by no one greater, He swore by Himself, saying, "Surely blessing I will bless you, and multiplying I will multiply you."And so, after he had patiently endured, he obtained the promise." Hebrews 6:15

Too many desire the promise without the process, but this is not the way of God. We want everything handed to us on a silver platter, as if salvation gives us some sort of privilege to escape true, authentic transformation in Christ. If we desire to receive that which God has stored up for His children, then we must expect to go through the process.

"But he who did not know, yet committed things deserving of stripes, shall be beaten with few. For everyone to whom much is given, from him much will be required; and to whom much has been committed, of him they will ask the more." Luke 12:48

The reason we have access to God today is because our Lord Jesus Christ understood that for the entire world to be saved, much would be required of Him. We desire promotions, elevation, recognition, and all of the other perks of ministry, yet we are not willing to suffer anything for the cause of Christ. We have to suffer through some things, in order for our character to be transformed into the image of Christ. It is only then that we are qualified to stand in His stead in the earth realm. We cannot stand in our flesh and call ourselves children of God. We must be changed for His glory! When it ceases to become about us, then we are ready to receive the *Promise*, because it is attached to others. The gifts of God within you are for the encouraging, equipping, exhorting, and empowering of those in your circle of influence.

God has breathed purpose into your life! Your gifts are lying dormant within you waiting to be stirred up and released, so the Kingdom of God can be released through you. How long will you settle for the mediocre in your life when God has magnificent plans that include you? How long will you sit back and watch other Believers prospering in their gifts, while you wallow on the sidelines of your faith? Do not allow your gift to waste away. We seek God for many things in life from our spouse, children, job, careers, home, cars, and other things, but until we lay aside our wants and desires and seek His Will, our destiny will never be birthed! You are not living life until you are walking in the predestined purposes of God; His Will. If we believe that He created us, then we must also believe that there is a plan already set in motion concerning our lives. He is the only One who truly knows the real Us! All we have to do is step into that *promise* and allow Him to lead us and direct us the entire way. We must press toward Him through His Son, Jesus Christ, who enduring persecution, humility, and suffering, made His way to the cross and became the *Promise* of our salvation.

I encourage you today, if you are not sure of why you are here or what God's plan is for you in this earth, seek Him wholeheartedly right now. Whatever you have done up until this point in your life, put it behind you and press forward! He accepts us where we are and does not wait for us to get it all together before He will begin to release the *promises* to us. You can be ten or one-hundred and ten; it does not matter your age, but your commitment to obey. Abraham was one-hundred years old when his son Isaac was born. (Genesis 21:5) It is never too late to release the *promise*, our destiny, into our lives. It does not matter whether you are homeless or if you live in a mansion; if you do not know God as your Father, Jesus as your personal Savior, and Holy Spirit as your Teacher, you will never receive the *Promise* that God desires for you here in the earth.

Far too many that have achieved great success in the world cannot come to terms with this Truth. They have accumulated great wealth and status and somehow feel they are above a relationship with Jesus Christ. They believe their "good works" alone will get them into Heaven. They do not understand that worldly promises are not eternal promises. Worldly promises are temporary and will fade away. They also come with great consequences.

"For what profit is it to a man if he gains the whole world, and loses his own soul? Or what will a man give in exchange for his soul?" Matthew 16:26

Do not expect God to release anything to you, unless you have made an honest commitment to die to yourself and pick up your cross and follow Him…wholeheartedly! Faith is one of the keys of the Kingdom that releases the *promise* of God in our lives. God responds to faith… period. Faith is the only thing that pleases our Father in Heaven. If we are not seeking Him with genuine, authentic faith, then we must examine ourselves.

"And He said, 'I will hide my face from them, I will see what their end will be, For they are a perverse generation, Children in whom is no faith." Deuteronomy 32:20

God is able to discern between the real and the fake; the authentic and the counterfeit. He is the only wise God; the Omnipotent, Omniscient, Omnipresent God; the All Knowing, All Seeing, Everywhere at All times God. We cannot pull anything over on Him. He knows where each of us stands in our walk with Him. Until we make up in our minds to walk in faith and trust in Him, we will continue to go in circles, as the children of Israel did in the wilderness. Too many are dying in their "wilderness," because they refuse to humble themselves and hear the voice of Holy Spirit leading, guiding, and directing them. As we heed His voice, He will bring the proper transformation needed to lead us into the *promises* of God for our lives. We serve a God who is able to see each and every person He ever created at the same time, no matter what time zone they are in, because there is no time in Him. At the very moment each one of us submits and surrenders to His Will, there is activation in the spiritual realm. Faith is released! The

Word says He gives each of us a measure of faith, according to the grace of God.

Many believe they are walking in faith, yet continue to allow worry and doubt to overtake their thoughts. We don't have to know everything concerning our gifts and/or assignment. All we need is simple, mustard-seed faith and God will honor it. It is time for us to fully surrender to His plan, so He is able to use us for His glory. We must die daily to our own selfish agendas and fall flat on our faces, so He can lift us up in His truth. As long as we are the focus of "our" success, God can never release His full plan for our lives. We must become broken before the Lord, so He is able to effectively use us in the Kingdom.

. I have seen throughout my life how merciful of a God I serve and how He has revealed Himself to me. I am who I am, simply because of Him. He desires to release His *promises* over our lives, but we must obey His Word. The gifts within you are a *promise* from Him. But again, many have refused and rejected this truth. How many are truly walking in their God-ordained gifts and/or assignments? I had to go through many tests and trials, sometimes great adversity even at a young age, but God was with me. I still had to experience life; I was not exempt from it simply because I was now a Believer in Christ Jesus. In fact, much of what we go through is part of the process of preparation for the *Promise* of God in our lives. I went through the preparation in the wilderness times, which laid the foundation for my walk with the Lord. Through the obedience of other Believers, I was *persuaded* to turn fully to God in submission and surrender. Once I made this commitment, God began to release His blessing over my life, which led to great *producing* of fruit in my life... fruit that would remain. After receiving, accepting, and acknowledging Holy Spirit in my life, I found out how to *protect* the gifts on the inside of me through wisdom and understanding. I allowed Holy Spirit to lead and guide me to where God wanted me to go. This level in my walk with the Lord led me into the *profiting* stage, where others were now seeing fruit in their lives through the witness of my testimony, and the power of God's Word preached.

God was now using His gifts within me to bring others into His saving knowledge. What a joy it is to walk in the Will of God for your life! There is no greater joy! When you are led by the Spirit of God, you can never go wrong. God's perfect Will for your life is released through the guidance of Holy Spirit. Once I made it a habit of seeking Holy Spirit, God began to open His gifts within me in greater capacities. He pushed me toward the *Promise* through the very act of obeying His voice. If we cannot obey His voice, then we cannot and will not be trusted with Kingdom treasures.

Obedience is another key to unlocking the *promises* of God in our lives. Can God trust you to keep His commandments? Can He release the keys to the Kingdom to you? We must daily examine ourselves to be sure we are still in the Will of our Father. The Word of God is our mirror. If we read the Word and see something lacking in our lives, then it is our responsibility to practice it until it becomes a part of us. This Word must become flesh; it has to be so ingrained within us that others can read the Word and see us! We are called to be living epistles, read by men.

Once I began to obey His voice, without any motive or intention, He began to open up His gifts within me. I was content with where I was in Him. I simply desired to intercede as Holy Spirit led me, and there was nothing else I sought from the Lord. But there was more HE had purposed within me, and He began to reveal it day by day. God knew what He created in me and His plans for my life were much more than I could ever think with my limited wisdom and understanding. Just as David reveals in the following Psalm, there is nothing hidden from God:

"For You formed my inward parts; You covered me in my mother's womb. I will praise You, for I am fearfully and won-derfully made; Marvelous are your works, and that my soul knows very well. My frame was not hidden from You, when I was made in secret, and skillfully wrought in the lowest parts of the earth. Your eyes saw my substance, being yet unformed, and in Your book they were all written, the days fashioned for me, when as yet there were none of them." Psalm 139:13-16

This scripture is probably one of the most inspiring scriptures in the Word! David praises the Lord for His marvelous creation, David himself. He is glorying God for His absolute power in the forming of his life. I had to come to a point of believing this for my own life, as well. We all have a *promise* from God and within that promise; He has released gifts to each of us, in order to fulfill His ultimate plan in the earth. The promises of this world are if and maybe, which are risky and unprofitable. The *Promises* of God are *Yes* and *Amen*, to the glory of God, which are *faithful* and *eternal*. Receive them today and allow Him to *Stir Up the Gift* in your life!

7

The Power of Purpose

Our walk with Christ is much more than the promise of Heaven, salvation; it is the power to fulfill the very purpose for which we were created by God. God makes no mistakes. Every child conceived in their mother's womb was first conceived in the mind of God, with purpose. Don't walk through this life purposeless. Seek God with all of your heart as to what you are here for and who you have been called to reach for the glory of God. The enemy of our souls would love nothing more than to deceive us into thinking our lives are our own and that it is our right to live it how we choose. Once we surrender our lives to His Will, we are no longer our own. We are bought with a price, and no earthly treasure can serve as a replacement for such a sacrifice. We are now heirs with Christ Jesus and sons of God.

Upon establishing a kingdom, there were many rules and laws that had to be set in order. Many kingdoms operated on the lines of succession; as being the firstborn son of a king to succeed him. For many reasons, this route had to be changed because of either disgrace to the throne or through death. Children born to kings are raised, if you will, to inherit their father's kingdom. They are groomed from infancy to take on a role that was chosen for them by their parents before they were even birthed into this world. There are no choices for these children, so they eventually step into their assigned positions. Their entire lives are mapped out for them, so they can move freely into their roles.

These children are taught their purpose early on in their lives, so they will not have any outside influence that will deter them from fulfilling their obligation. They are conditioned to this purpose, therefore giving them a better chance to succeed in their future role as king. This is how God desires for us, as His sons, to inherit His Kingdom, through a line of succession that began with a promise to Abram.

"Then He brought him outside and said, 'Look now toward heaven, and count the stars if you are able to number them.'
"And He said to him, 'So shall your descendants be."
Genesis 15:5

God made a covenant with Abram that he would have many descendants. He changed his name to Abraham to signify the *Purpose* of this; he was to be a *father of many nations*. He produced two children, Ishmael, from his servant Hagar and Isaac, from his wife Sarah. We begin to see a distinguishing between his descendants; his son Isaac and his son Ishmael. God specifically tells Abraham that Ishmael will be blessed and multiplied exceedingly, but that His covenant lies with Isaac, who would be born to his wife, Sarah. So we see here that the line of succession did not go to Abraham's firstborn, but to Isaac, the son of *Promise*. God had a *purpose* for allowing Isaac to inherit Abraham's legacy and not Ishmael. Scripture reveals Sarah's lack of trust in God. She laughed at the messenger that told her she would conceive. In her natural mind, she was past the age of conception; therefore, she asked Abraham to go in to her maidservant Hagar to bear children with her.

We should never doubt God no matter how desolate our situation or circumstances may look to us. He is God! He can do the miraculous in our lives if we would simply believe and wait upon Him. Even after Sarah gave up on bearing her own children, she was given a promise by God that she would bear a son by Abraham. God had great *purpose* in revealing the proclamation before the process of preparation was complete. God wants to build our faith and trust in Him. He desires to form a deeply intimate relationship with His children, so we can partner with Him in the earth realm. True relationship is revealed when we cannot see the full outcome, but choose to walk through it anyway. Even after God changes our names, makes us new in Christ, we tend to choose doubt over faith. We must learn to trust Him and believe His Word. The purpose He created in us is far more complex than we can ever imagine. Abraham and Sarah did not quite realize the extent of the role God has *purposed* for them.

"No longer shall your name be called Abram, but your name shall be Abraham; for I have made you a father of many nations. I will make you exceedingly fruitful; and I will make nations of you, and kings shall come from you. And I will establish My covenant between Me and you and your descendants after you in their generations, for an everlasting covenant, to be God to you and your descendants after you." Genesis 17:5-7

This is powerful! God's plan for establishing His Kingdom here in the earth is connected to ordinary people like Abraham, Sarah, Isaac, and yes, even you and I. God created this *purpose* in us before we were found sinful; before we entered into this sinful world. His *purpose* is to bring us back to the Beginning, where He created and said it was "Good." Never downplay the role you play in God's master plan. His main *purpose* for you and I in this earth is to release His glory through our transformed lives. This is why He chooses to work through ordinary people to bring about extraordinary change, and this can only take place through His Son, Jesus Christ.

Holy Spirit revealed such a sweet revelation to me years ago. My life was never the same after hearing this. I knew God desired to use me, but I was not sure of exactly how? Several doors opened to me and I began to be obedient in those specific areas, waiting on the Father to release His perfect Will for my life. Well, in this time of opening doors to my *purpose*, my family's financial state seemed to be getting worse. I could not understand why, as God was opening doors, He would allow us to move backwards in an area that would only benefit the *purpose*. What I finally understood was that God releases His gifts, assignments, and calling into our lives without provision, so we will seek Him with our whole hearts. He will test us in every area to see where our motives lie. He will reveal if there are any hidden agendas in our lives. Many will move out on other things, because they feel God is taking too long, or that He is holding something back from us. Did Sarah feel this way concerning children? Have you ever felt this way, as God purposefully withheld something from you that you felt He should have released? This is probably the most crucial stage of God revealing His *purpose* to us. God is in no hurry. He desires to produce great character and integrity within us, as without these pertinent keys, our gifts can and will become perverted.

Too many gifted people in the Body of Christ have lost everything, because of selfish ambition and perverted desires. No matter what God releases to us, it is ultimately to bring glory to His name. Receive NOTHING unless it points back to the Lord. This is where many fall, because instead of seeking God for what He wants for our lives, we prematurely choose for ourselves what we think we want. Or we fall into envy, jealousy, and competition, seeking what others have. We fail to allow Holy Spirit to lead us in the direction of our lives. We refuse to consult the One who created us and knows our beginning from our end. Holy Spirit said to me, "Where am I receiving the glory in your life" We would rather allow people, and ourselves, to believe it is through our hard work, dedication, and commitment that we have the things we have. We ultimately steal the glory from God.

"And you shall remember the Lord your God, for it is He who gives you power to get wealth that He may establish His covenant which He swore to your fathers, as it is this day."
Deuteronomy 8:18

God says He will share His glory with no one! We deserve nothing that God has so mercifully and graciously extended to us. But simply because of His covenant with Abraham, He will stand over His Word to perform it in our lives. Whatever provision He does release to us is attached to His *purpose*, not our selfish agendas. The *purpose* for the gifts we possess must point back to Him, so His Kingdom is established within us. But again, far too many become impatient and seek outside of God's Will for acceptance and reward. The Body of Christ is losing so many to worldly influence, from pastors to psalmists. They have fallen prey to a celebrity-driven gospel that seeks to put them on pedestals and creates idols of them in the eyes of the Church. Their gifts are pimped and perverted, and it is no longer about establishing God's Kingdom, but their own selfish empires. Because of this, their only concern is the piling up of their gifts, while God's people sit in the church pews never realizing their purpose in the Kingdom. This is a devastating thing to see. As they continue in this downward spiral, the compromise leads them to partnering with the world to keep these empires flourishing. They no longer have the heart of a shepherd; they are now hirelings. If it does not produce something for their benefit, it is not worth their time. God help us!

God spoke to me ten years ago the phrase, "Stir Up the Gift". I began a conference based upon this title, believing this was what God was saying to me. A way to help others realize the gifts of God within them, and to encourage and support them in their endeavors. Well, this was what I was used to seeing others do in the Church, so I followed suit. It fell apart. It was not God's plan. Instead of waiting to hear the next step, I moved out too soon. As time passed, I began to see how the gifts in the Church were being stifled and not stirred up. This scripture God revealed to me, as the foundation for what He was speaking to me:

"Therefore I remind you to stir up the gift of God which is in you through the laying on of my hands." 2 Timothy 1:6

I have had several people lay their hands on me over the years to impart into me, as well as anoint me. I believe God still uses this method today, but I also believe it is one of the most abused. Far too many desire to be seen by others, instead of drawing upon the power of Holy Spirit and His leading in the lives of God's people. Nothing seems authentic any longer when it comes to releasing God's true servants into the work of the Kingdom. In fact, it is more like a "who's who" of the church world, instead of those that God is actually calling forth; those He has ordained, and not man. I have witnessed this with my own eyes over many years and it is a travesty. People are put into positions that God has not assigned them and it has brought great harm to the Church. My heart has been set on fire to encourage, exhort, equip, and empower my fellow brothers and sisters to *Stir up the Gift* of God within. With the rise in spiritual abuse within the Church, many are sitting in church pews day in and day out without recognizing the gifts inside of them. Power, control, manipulation, and intimidation have silenced God's people from even seeking what those gifts are, and if they do, they are rebuked! This is NOT God! It is God's desire that each of His children are walking in their God-ordained gifts and assignments. We are all to be functioning members of the Body of Christ, so God can come and do as He pleases amongst us.

"… from whom the whole body, joined and knit together by what every joint supplies, according to the effective working by which every part does its share, causes growth of the body for the edifying of itself in love." Ephesians 4:16

We have to be mindful not to allow one person, or a "clique" of people, to have too much control in any given arena, especially when it comes to the Body of Christ. Why? Because the spirit of control, manipulation, and intimidation sets out to stifle any voice that opposes doctrinal error and/or spiritual abuse within the Church. As all of God's people are operating in their respective gifts and/or assignments, Holy Spirit is able to freely test the atmosphere of any gathering. Prophets should be speaking one by one, not just one voice that does not get to be tested. Confirmations should come forth when God's people are operating in the Spirit. But too many are afraid to speak, because of the authoritarian spirit exuding from our pulpits! We need shepherds that are not covetous and envious of the gifts within the Body, those that are able to pull them out and stir up these precious souls for the work of the Kingdom!

The gifts within you were given to you specifically, according to your makeup; the way in which God created you. We can look at the setting of diamonds to reveal how God sees this process. As a jeweler sets precious diamonds into a piece of jewelry, he has to use a special tool that will insert the gem safely into its proper position, so there will be no chipping. He then set prongs, or guards, around the precious jewel to keep it from falling out of its proper place. After looking at his finished product, he buffs out the impurities caused by his continued work on the piece, and shines it up, so that it is presentable on display.

This is the same manner in which God takes care of the *purpose* He has placed inside of you and me. It is very precious to Him and because of that, He ensures that He will guard it and protect it at all costs. We do not have to do anything but obey His Word and He will do the rest. It is not about what you will do to accomplish the goal, but what He has already done in you for the furthering of His Kingdom. I fully believe this is where we often fall short. We assume it is something we are called to finish, when He has already stated, "It is finished!" He has already done the work on the Cross. It was all completed at Calvary. All we need to do is walk in it and flow in the gifts He has already perfected within us. Our process, as we spoke of earlier, is a crucial key to walking in this authority. If we skip this process, then we have no right to walk in our gifting. Though He has finished it, we, as earthly beings, MUST be transformed by His Word and by His Spirit, or we will hurt many people. Allow the work of the Lord to be completed within you.

Our *purpose* and our gifts are always attached to other people. God will send people into our lives during different seasons to mentor, to impart, to share, and to encourage us in our assignments. Their experience is crucial to the development in our own assignments. I know this is a much abused area, as many that are spiritual mentors cross boundaries and step into areas that are only reserved for God alone. But as we submit to Holy Spirit, God will use us in the lives of others to help them along their journey. One such mentor, a very wise man, once told me, "Deborah, we are to hold very loosely God's people. They are not ours; they are His." I held this very close to me, because I have witnessed great control and manipulation from spiritual leadership. Leaders, please only lead as the Lord directs you in people's lives. We do not own them, and we are not called to control the gifts in their lives. Let God use you to bless them and equip them to walk in their designed *purpose*. Remember, you are not God; you are merely a vessel He may use in their lives.

Another crucial aspect of walking in your *purpose* as a Believer in Christ Jesus is understanding that we are not called to infiltrate the world with our gifts. The Word of God says that we are to be a light to them, so that they will see our good works and glorify Him in Heaven. They should be coming to us, not us to them. This is one of the greatest tricks of the enemy in the lives of God's people today. So many say God is calling them into Hollywood, yet they end up compromising and falling into great temptation. We must read and heed the Word of God and stop making it say what it does not say. God tells us to separate ourselves from the world. Meaning, light and darkness have no fellowship together. We are called to love and pray for the world, but we are NOT called to mingle within their circles. We see so many pastors, ministers, psalmists, and musicians within the Church hanging out at awards shows, walking on red carpets, taking photos in front of billboards, and taking selfies with superstars. What is the *purpose?* When we allow ourselves to get in these atmospheres, we allow the spirit upon it to get on us. Then, we twist the Word of God to suit our own selfish desires and deceive ourselves into thinking this is what He wants for His children. He DOES NOT contradict Himself. His Word DOES NOT lie and it is very dangerous to manipulate it to suit our sinful nature. The wisdom of the Word guards us against the deception of this world. If we choose to ignore it, we will surely face the consequences of that disobedience. Walk circumspectly and allow Holy Spirit to lead you, as you fulfill God's assignment in your life.

As you continue to bathe yourself in the Word of God and are blanketed by the leading of Holy Spirit, God will begin to open up the gifts and assignment in your life. When, or if, another person comes to prophesy what God has called you to do, there should be confirmation in your spirit. You should already know what the Lord has called you to do, as you have spent intimate time in His presence. This is where responsibility will come on your part, not the part of the messenger. If someone speaks something into your life that is not true, DO NOT receive it! I have seen way too many people accept titles, gifts, assignments, and/or positions that God did not release to them. You ask how I know. The fruit will always reveal.

God says He gives us shepherds after His own heart. When I see "pastors" that are prideful, arrogant, condescending, sarcastic, demeaning, and downright ugly towards God's people, I know, by their fruit, their hearts are not after His. Many have taken on a job, not an assignment from the Lord. I have seen "prophets" that are quick to prophesy cars, homes, jobs, spouses, children, money, and influence… the blessing of God into the lives of rebellious and disobedient people. I know they are not speaking for Him. They are itching the ears of people that merely want you to tell them what they want to hear. And many other self-proclaimed "prophets" are prophesying outrageous things that never come to pass! Yet, we continue to call them prophets and continue to put them on platforms for millions to be deceived. We have to have accountability restored to the Church, where these imposters are confronted and removed from these positions.

We understand that the five-fold ministry gifts (Apostle, Prophet, Evangelist, Pastor, and Teacher) are New Testament offices, set by God for the edifying of the Body of Christ. But what we have failed to discern and manage is who has been called and who has not.

"And He Himself gave some to be apostles, some prophets, some evangelists, and some pastors and teachers, for the equipping of the saints for the work of ministry, for the edifying of the body of Christ, till we all come to the unity of the faith and of the knowledge of the Son of God, to a perfect man, to the measure of the stature of the fullness of Christ; that we should no longer be children, tossed to and fro and carried about with every wind of doctrine, by the trickery of men, in the cunning craftiness of deceitful plotting, but, speaking the truth in love, may grow up in all things into Him who is the head—Christ— from whom the whole body, joined and knit together by what every joint supplies, according to the effective working by which every part does its share, causes growth of the body for the edifying of itself in love." Ephesians 4:11-16

The key word in this scripture is *some*. These days, everyone you see has a five-fold ministry title. Many insist you call them by their title, or they become offended? These people are not called by God; they have called themselves. The most authentic ministry gifts I have been privileged to meet have NEVER put a title in front of their names. They simply introduce themselves by their first name. Again, the fruit will reveal itself. Your gifts themselves will introduce you, not a proclamation of who you say you are. So many people are out of their assigned positions in the Kingdom due to covetousness and envy. I am sorry, but I refuse to accept an assignment God did not give me. How many people can be harmed deeply by me taking a position I was not graced by God to complete? I was approached several times to start my own church. I laughed, because if I know anything, I KNOW God has not called me to shepherd anyone! Yes, I have great compassion for God's people, but He has not called me to be anyone's pastor. I was grateful that I knew who I was and what God has called me to do for His Kingdom. We must be grounded, so we can hear what He is saying to us. And we must seek discernment to know who we are "sitting" under. Has God called them to pastor His people? Has God called them to be His mouthpiece? Has He called them to evangelize the world? Has He called them to plant and build? Has He called them to teach? We can know these things without a shadow of a doubt if we would simply ask Holy Spirit to reveal it to us. May we stop so quickly ordaining people and get back to Biblical fasting and praying and seeking God's wisdom in this area. I believe He is restoring this greatly. He is removing those *man* has ordained and lifting up those He has called! Glory to God!

Now to those that know and understand they are not called within the five-fold ministry, what are your gifts? What is that pull in your spirit that you cannot seem to ignore? What produces passion within you? What can you do for the Lord without getting paid to do it? I know I might lose some here. Yes, God provides certain talents and abilities that we are to prosper financially from and this is His desire, but the test is what are we willing to do in the Kingdom that we expect no compensation?

Again, it is not that God will not add things to us, but what are we seeking first? Are we seeking the precious souls that will come to know Him, or are we calculating how much money we will bring home from a ministry event? These are real questions that need to be addressed. We have reduced the Gospel to prosperity the world's way and have perverted the name of our Lord. We must repent and turn back to our first love. As we wholeheartedly seek Him for our *purpose* in life, He will reveal it to us. It is not revealed in its fullness, so we must be patient and wait on Him; trust Him. Make loving people and leading them to Christ be our first priority. Don't allow the enemy to deceive you into putting yourself and your desires above God's Will. It will surely lead to destruction. As you allow God to produce brokenness, humility, submission, surrender, and obedience in your life, then He is able to release the treasures of the Kingdom.

I encourage you this day to seek God for your *purpose*. Trust the Lord your God who created you with beautiful gifts and needs you to operate in them to further His Kingdom in the earth. No matter what path life takes you down, know that God has a plan for you and it will succeed, as you submit and surrender to His Will. It has not changed. People need what is inside of you! Nations and generations have the potential to be changed by what is within each of us. There will be great tests, trials, suffering, adversity, and persecution, but count it all joy! Nothing in God is birthed without each of these, in some way, affecting our lives. Many give up on the process, because it hurts too much. Take it from me, this is by no means an easy walk, but it was never intended to be so. We need to be willing to travail in the Spirit for the *purpose* in which we were created. Do not settle for the easy way out; God is not in the business of simply giving out gifts. He is more interested in transforming our lives for His glory, so others can see it and seek Him, as well.

Your revelation of who Jesus Christ is in your life will not only determine if you receive the keys to the Kingdom, but it will also determine how you see yourself and the gifts God has placed within you.

"And I also say to you that you are Peter, and on this rock I will build my church, and the gates of Hades shall not prevail against it. And I will give you the keys of the kingdom of heaven, and whatever you bind on earth will be bound in heaven, and whatever you loose on earth will be loosed in heaven"
Matthew 16:18-19

Peter received the revelation that Jesus was the Christ; the Son of the Living God and because of this, God pronounced that his name was no longer Simon, but Peter. He was now walking in his ordained purpose; receiving the very keys to the Kingdom of God. It is only when we understand He is God and that Jesus died on the Cross for our sins, that our purpose is released. Our gifts and assignment lies IN Him and cannot be separated from Him. We can utilize our natural gifts and talents any day and even prosper in them, but the spiritual gifts we possess cannot and will not be released, until we have been prepared by the Lord.

Allow your gifts the opportunity to grow and be developed by God, so He is able to use you for His glory. The Kingdom of God is surely at hand and our world is growing darker by the day. This world needs what is inside of you and me. They are hungering and thirsting for an answer, and you are that answer! Your transformed life has the power to bring many other souls into His Kingdom. If we are to call ourselves followers of Jesus Christ, then we must be willing to lay down our lives, so that others may live. He is our perfect example!

"So Jesus answered and said, 'Assuredly, I say to you, there is no one who has left house or brothers or sisters or father or mother or wife or children or lands, for My sake and the gospel's, who shall not receive a hundredfold now in this time-houses and brothers and sisters and mothers and children and lands, with persecutions-and in the age to come, eternal life.'"
Mark 10:29-30

Deborah G. Hunter

"Many are called, but few are chosen." (Matthew 22:14) Please know that not many are truly walking in their God-ordained assignments today. Many are not in their proper positions in Christ. Many are trespassing in others' gifts and callings, because they have yet to know who they were created to be, and many are being harmed in the Church. We must understand that we are at war with the kingdom of darkness and our enemy's number one tool is deceit. Many today are deceiving and being deceived. Separate yourself from the world and separate yourself unto the Lord, so you are able to hear His voice clearly. Allow Him to *Stir Up the Gift* of God within you, so you can be a part of the great harvest of souls in the earth realm! I am standing with you and praying earnestly for you my brothers and sisters!

About the Author

Deborah G. Hunter is a wife, mother, author, inspirational speaker, and CEO & Publisher of Hunter Heart Publishing, and co-owner of Hunter Entertainment Network. She has written six books of her own, Breaking the Eve Mentality, Raising Your Prophet, The Call of Intercession, The Wilderness, El Desierto, and her new bestseller Holy Spirit, The Promise Left for the Believer. Deborah travels nationally & internationally on her mission to "Offer God's Heart to a Dying World" through the inspired gift of writing, personal testimony, and through the gifts God has placed within her. She serves as an avid philanthropist through her charity, *Stir Up the Gift*, dedicated to providing support for the needy around the world, including the country of Japan after the wake of the 2011 Earthquake/Tsunami that ravaged this country.

Deborah has been a born-again believer since the age of twelve and has been on her pathway to destiny ever since. She was ordained as a Minister in Prophetic Gifting on July 7, 2007 in Kitzingen, Germany from International Gospel Church. She received her Bachelor's of Arts Degree in Biblical Studies/Theology, Magna Cum Laude, from Minnesota Graduate School of Theology in 2009.

Deborah is married to Chris Hunter, Jr., radio personality and CEO of Hunter Entertainment Network, a conglomerate of Christian media outlets, including record label, movie, book, and music production companies. They share in the raising of their three children together, Jade, Elijah, and Ja'el, and are the father and step-mother of three, along with three beautiful grandchildren. They reside in the beautiful mountains of Colorado.

OTHER BOOKS BY
DEBORAH G. HUNTER

THE WILDERNESS SERIES

COMING SOON!

website: hunter-entertainment.com
Facebook: Deborah G. Hunter
Twitter: @hunterheartpub
YouTube: Hunter Heart Publishing

OTHER BOOKS BY
DEBORAH G. HUNTER

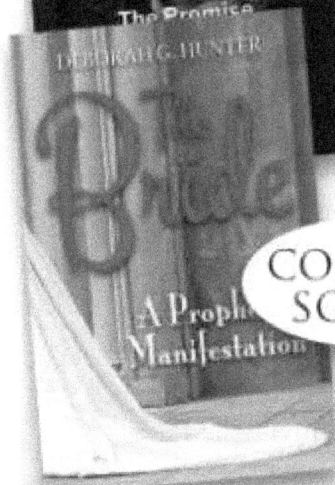

Holy
SPIRIT

The Promise

STIR UP
THE GIFT

The Journey to

DEBORAH G. HUNTER

Bride

A Prophetic
Manifestation

the
elephant
in the room

EXPOSING THE EVIL
OF SPIRITUAL ABUSE

Deborah G Hunter

COMING
SOON!

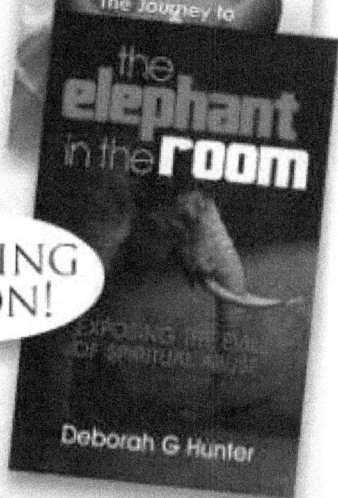

website: hunter-entertainment.com
Facebook: Deborah G. Hunter
Twitter: @hunterheartpub
YouTube: Hunter Heart Publishing

Stir Up the Gift

By: Sean A. Goode

The heavens have never looked so big nor the road so long
Staring eternity in the eye while hope holds on
Praying to God I know life means more than this
So many goals and dreams Lord, please Stir up the Gift

Tried to do it, all alone so many times
Blind leading the blind becoming a mime
Of dreamers past who failed to wake and walk out life
Preferring the darkness of night to the new day, your Son's
light

A firm grip upon the stars where wishes were born
This ship that sails followed them right through the storm
Now God says it is time to let them go
Set your sails on high, as I will be the wind that blows

Destination set, but yet the steps never seem clear
One moment they're there, the next they quickly disappear
The road is narrow, but You promise to lead the way
Not by sight, but by Your Spirit; moving by faith

If this is the way to see the purpose that You gave
Lord take this life, from here on out, I am Your slave
To righteousness, to love, for salvation's sake
If I die before I wake, I pray my soul You take

Either way this vessel is Yours, do as You wish
No more waiting; drop the nets and pull up the fish

Not just enough, but running over; this Your promise is
Let your Word cleanse this heart and be upon these lips
Speaking those things that are not as though they were
Allowing miracles to happen, Your glory observed
So that those who did not know would come to believe
That they too could find the strength in You to live their goals
and dreams

The heavens have never looked so big nor the road so long
Staring eternity in the eye while hope holds on
Praising God I now know life means more than this
Lord here I am, Your humble servant… Stir up the Gift!

www.ingramcontent.com/pod-product-compliance
Lightning Source LLC
LaVergne TN
LVHW051420080426
835508LV00022B/3170